FUNDAMENTALISM
in
American Religion
1880 - 1950

A forty-five-volume facsimile series
reproducing often extremely rare material
documenting the development of one of the
major religious movements of our time

■ *Edited by*
Joel E. Carpenter
Billy Graham Center, Wheaton College
■ *Advisory Editors*
Donald W. Dayton,
Northern Baptist Theological Seminary
George M. Marsden,
Duke University
Mark A. Noll,
Wheaton College
Grant Wacker,
University of North Carolina

A GARLAND SERIES

■ The Old Fashioned
Revival Hour
and the
Broadcasters

J. Elwin Wright

Garland Publishing, Inc.
New York & London
1988

For a list of titles in this series, see the final pages of this volume.
This facsimile has been made from a copy at the
Billy Graham Center of Wheaton College.

Library of Congress Cataloging-in-Publication Data

Wright, J. Elwin.
    The Old Fashioned Revival Hour and the broadcasters / J.
Elwin Wright.
        p. cm. — (Fundamentalism in American religion, 1880-
1950)
        Reprint. Originally published: Boston, Mass. : Fellowship
Press, 1940.
        ISBN 0-8240-5040-1 (alk. paper)
        1. Fuller, Charles Edward, 1887-1968. 2. Evangelists—
United States—Biography. 3.   Old Fashioned Revival
Hour (Radio program)
        4. Radio in religion—United States. I. Title. II. Series.
        BV3785.F8W7 1988
        262' .2' 0924—dc 19   88-4131
        [B]   CIP

Design by Valerie Mergentime
Printed on acid-free, 250-year-life paper
Manufactured in the United States of America

EDITOR'S NOTE

■ This lively gospel radio program featured Charles E. Fuller (1887–1968), a fundamentalist preacher from California. By the late 1930s, the "Old-Fashioned Revival Hour" was a program on the Mutual Broadcasting System, and Fuller was a religious celebrity. He drew huge urban crowds to the "radio rallies" of his coast-to-coast preaching tours. This breezy account documents the style of Fuller's broadcast, offers a selection of listeners' letters, and shows the ties between the resurgence of evangelical Christianity and fundamentalists' skillful use of religious broadcasting.

J.A.C.

THE

OLD FASHIONED

REVIVAL HOUR

and the

Broadcasters

*

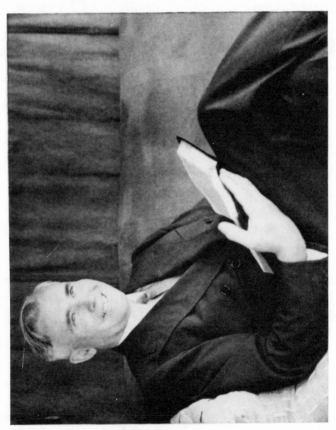

MR. FULLER FEASTS ON GOD'S WORD

THE
OLD FASHIONED REVIVAL
HOUR
and the Broadcasters

by

J. Elwin Wright

President
New England Fellowship

THE FELLOWSHIP PRESS

5 PARK STREET, BOSTON, MASS.

TO

MRS. LEONORA BARNHILL

WHOM WE HAVE NEVER MET

BUT HAVE LEARNED TO LOVE

FOR HER IMPORTANT PART

IN THIS MINISTRY

CONTENTS

7

CONTENTS

LIST OF ILLUSTRATIONS

ACKNOWLEDGEMENTS

We acknowledge with deep appreciation the courtesies shown us by Mr. and Mrs. Charles E. Fuller in making available to us photographs, letters and data which were indispensable in the preparation of this volume.

We are also greatly indebted to Dr. Charles G. Trumbull for the use of material and to Rev. and Mrs. Cutler B. Whitwell for their valuable suggestions.

The assistance of the Misses Elizabeth M. Evans and Kathryn M. Evans in the gathering and preparation of material has been an invaluable aid.

THE AUTHOR

INTRODUCTION

THE STORY of the Old Fashioned Revival Hour is one of the most amazing miracles of God's grace and power in the field of Christian evangelism during our lifetime. There seems to be nothing else quite like it. There are many other truly sound and evangelistic broadcasts in North America, some covering a wide range; but I know of no other fundamental, evangelistic broadcast filling a full hour in the heart of Sunday evening that is nation-wide and coast-to-coast, reaching out also to the southernmost tip of South America and to islands of the sea, as the divinely empowered Old Fashioned Revival Hour is doing. It stands uncompromisingly for the whole Bible as the Word of God, the Lord Jesus Christ as the only Saviour of lost sinners, His virgin birth, the blood atonement of His substitutionary and sacrificial death on the cross, His bodily resurrection, the work of the Holy Spirit in making Christ known to men and bringing to pass in them the new birth through faith in Christ, and

13

the imminent, premillennial return of Christ to establish
His Kingdom on earth.

Mr. Fuller would be the first to disclaim that the reach
and blessing of this broadcast is to be accounted for by
any eloquence or power of his as a preacher and exposi-
tor. He is a simple-hearted, straightforward business man
and layman at heart, although, after years in the business
world, when he was saved he took a thorough training
in the Bible Institute of Los Angeles, and later was ordained as a minister. But he is a patient, thorough, untir-
ing student of God's Word. He knows how to dig deep
in the riches of the Bible, and how to bring forth and
share with others the treasures he finds there. He "knows
folks," and he and his wife, having turned their lives over
to the Lord in full surrender and dedication years ago,
have as their supreme interest and passion today the giving of the gospel to the uncounted millions of lost souls
in North America, and the building up, in Christ and the
Word, of God's people throughout the land.

Mr. Fuller's evangelistic messages and Bible teaching
are simple, direct, straightforward, carefully planned and
well worked out, and they go straight to the hearts of
people who want Christ and the gospel and Bible training
—also they go straight to the hearts of many who think
they *don't* want Christ and the gospel at all, but whom
God reaches, in spite of themselves, through the Old
Fashioned Revival Hour.

How it all came about is told in the story of the broadcast and of the devoted man and woman who have been

called of God to this great ministry, and who have let God work out His plans in and through them for the salvation and establishing of countless souls.

If ever the world needed such a ministry, it is today. Surely God is showing us again that "when the enemy shall come in like a flood, the Spirit of the Lord shall lift up a standard against him" (Isaiah 59:19).

CHARLES G. TRUMBULL

PRELUDE

I HAD TO kill a man. Is there any redemption for a killer? I will be in another State by Sunday night but will hear your voice in my car radio."

This letter, headed "On the road," was in the morning mail at the office of Charles E. Fuller, in Pasadena, on a November morning.

Because Mr. Fuller has the answer to a question like this, thousands of people are baring their hearts in letters which require the services of fifteen people to read, classify, answer, and follow up with prayer and helpful suggestions.

The Old Fashioned Revival Hour, conducted by Mr. Fuller and his associates, has become, without doubt, one of the greatest evangelizing agencies of the present generation. Every Sunday night, several million people sit by their radios in their homes, in pastorless churches, in their automobiles, in hospitals and sanatoriums, in prisons, in restaurants and even in saloons while they listen to a service which is so simple that a child of six can understand, so heart-warming that bankers, surgeons, and educators follow it eagerly, and yet so instructive that the lives of thousands are being revolutionized by listening.

Charles E. Fuller is propagating no new religion; he is not proposing some new system of metaphysics nor founding a new cult. He is not a great preacher, if by preaching one means ability to be oratorical, but he speaks plainly, convincingly, and sincerely, out of a full heart.

When "Snow White and the Seven Dwarfs" became the talk of the Nation, some time ago, one nationally known critic exclaimed, in an ecstasy of enthusiasm, "It is the happiest thing that has happened since the World War."

I beg to differ. It is my sincere belief that the happiest thing since the World War is the Old Fashioned Revival Hour, because it has helped a considerable portion of the Nation to re-discover something of which it had lost sight.

This broadcast, winging its way across the continent to the eastward and over the vast stretches of the Pacific Ocean to the westward, deals not with fairies or fanciful fables, but with facts, the knowledge or ignorance of which are a matter of life and death.

The cry out of the darkness, "Is there any redemption for a killer?" needs something more than sanctimonious platitudes. If there is no redemption our civilization is a farce. If there is, not only those who have killed their fellow men by physical violence but those who, because of hatred in their hearts, have become killers in the sight of God desperately need to know the way out.

The essence of the doctrine which is being proclaimed on the Old Fashioned Revival Hour is nothing more nor less than the doctrine which has been the foundation of every Christian organization on the face of the earth from the time of Christ down to the present. And this doctrine can be summed up in the two words which are the title of the Theme Song of this broadcast: "Jesus Saves."

1

A GLIMPSE OF THE FULLERS AT HOME

D RIVING ALONG an avenue of oaks and tropical ver-
dure, with the towering, wide-branched trees providing a lovely green canopy for the street, we come
almost abruptly to a driveway leading to an attractive
English, washed-brick home, the residence of Rev. and
Mrs. Charles E. Fuller. Sycamores shade the lawn and a
lovely flower bed at the farther end holds our attention
for a moment of real pleasure.

The inside of this attractive but unpretentious home
is furnished in good taste, in keeping with the exterior.
We are warmly welcomed by our most charming hostess,
who takes her place on a low seat near the fireplace while
we are made comfortable in chairs beside the library
table.

The house has a homey, used appearance, as though
those who live here love to slip away from a busy world
and find rest and refreshment within its walls; as though
love and understanding too, are found here. We are re-

minded of the words of the poet, "It takes a heap of living in a house to make a home." This is very evidently a place where there has been a lot of living.

"Now tell us, please, all about yourselves, and how the 'miracle broadcast' was started in the first place."

Mr. Fuller is nowhere in sight and it is well he is not, for we have found him ever reluctant to speak of himself and of his experiences. His reticence is well known among his friends—and appreciated. His charming wife shares his earnest desire that the Lord alone shall receive all the praise and glory for the wonderful work which is being done, and they are reluctant to relate even the incidents we feel their listening audience would like to hear regarding their early life, their conversion, and the opening days of the great drama of a coast-to-coast hookup of radio stations presenting a program more widely heard than almost any other program on the air today.

But, finally, we are launched on the recital. Mrs. Fuller is a woman of unusual charm and grace. Her large and expressive eyes gleam occasionally with humor. Her pleasingly musical voice waxes enthusiastic as she pictures, in the course of her narrative, victories won for the Lord, or grows tender with reminiscence, or carries an undertone of suffering as she remembers some time of keen sorrow, rising again to tones of triumph and of joy as she recalls the goodness of God and the conquests which He has made. Her expressive face is worth watching as she pours forth the details of this wonderful story.

22

It is a never-to-be-forgotten morning, a rare and deeply appreciated privilege.

Suddenly the house wakes up with a glad greeting. Mr. Fuller has returned from the office after a busy morning. He drops into a chair and, as we look into his face, we see there not only goodness, honesty and strength of character, but we see also the strain of difficult hours, the effects of discouragement and criticism and heavy burdens. For this man whose voice is heard every Sunday evening with a glad message of salvation and of hope, for everyone who will listen, carries a great load, a tremendous financial responsibility which only God can help him to bear from day to day. This load is not lightened but rather increased by those who fail to understand, who criticise and carp and hinder. We long to drop on our knees and help him carry this burden to the Throne, finding there relief and renewed strength, but our time is limited and there is much we want to hear. So, while our hostess slips away to prepare lunch, we question Mr. Fuller about the early days of his Christian ministry, the first broadcasts, and the outlook for the future. Diffidently, drawn out with a poised pencil and occasional questions, he gives us a word picture of some incidents of the past.

Soon we are called to lunch. To our surprise and delight we are ushered out into the warm October sunshine, to a lovely spot on the lawn where a colorful garden greatly contributes to our enjoyment of a tastily served meal. As our heads are bowed, Mr. Fuller leads us to the

Throne in a warm, brief prayer, and there follows an hour of sweet fellowship. The cares of the day are dropped, and the goodness of the Lord and the wonders of His grace occupy our conversation. The flowers are bright about us, the sycamores wide spreading and picturesque, with eucalyptus and palms in the distance, the near-by house brilliant in the sunshine.

But Mr. Fuller must hurry back to the office with copy for the next Heart-to-Heart Talk. He and Mrs. Fuller look it over together, making a correction here and there. We take a movie shot of the dear English home and its lovely hostess, watch Dan, the tall son of the family, hurry off to school on his bicycle, and settle down for further details of this fascinating story.

As we speak with admiration of the attractive home, Mrs. Fuller looks lovingly about her and says, "I feel as though it is my dear father's provision for us. Through the depression period it looked as though the money which he had left me was vanishing into thin air. But, almost miraculously, there was a recovery of some funds. With them we were able to purchase this little home, and we like to remember that this place where we may find rest and quietness is from him."

Later in the afternoon, Mr. Fuller returns and takes us all to the scene of his daily labors, the official home of the Gospel Broadcasting Association. Here, just north of the business district of Pasadena, in a neat, two-story, brick building we find three offices, a store room and a garage. The offices are a beehive of activity, for the Heart-to-

CHARLES E. FULLER

At nine months   At four and a half
A boy of fourteen   Graduating from college
As a young pastor

GRACE PAYTON FULLER

At five months   At two years old
With her grandmother   Eleven years old
Wife of the Placentia pastor

Heart Talks are being mailed to sixty-five thousand friends eagerly awaiting them; secretaries are opening letters pouring into the office requesting spiritual assistance or recounting blessing received from the broadcasts, or sending in contributions to help carry on this great work. Downstairs, mail bags are piled up ready to be taken to the post office. In the front office upstairs, to the left, is the room where Mr. Fuller personally answers thousands of requests for spiritual counsel. To the right is a long office where several girls are busily working at desks. Downstairs is a large room where an addressograph quickly types envelopes addressed to many thousands of friends. Some are working on the file, others are folding, still others are watching the machines at work.

We pause for a moving picture of the building and are taken on a brief sightseeing tour of Pasadena and surrounding towns. Then we return to the Fuller home and settle down for more inspiration; just a few more stories of God's wonderful grace and power. How we enjoy looking over the quaint baby pictures of this dear couple. We see the lines of strength and courage begin to deepen on the face of the earnest boy of fourteen, dressed in his very correct Y. M. C. A. uniform of that period. We study, with interest, the face of the young pastor of the Placentia church and his attractive wife, and are shown a studio pose, as well. I'm sure you wish to see these pictures, too, and you shall.

As we talk together how often our hearts overflow with praise to our heavenly Father while Mrs. Fuller recounts experiences which we realize were part of God's training in the lives of the two who carry forward this great work of broadcasting the gospel to millions of souls each week. But you must hear this story for yourself, and see the hand of God in the heritage and even in the severe testings of the two important characters of this narrative.

2

PARENTAGE, BIRTH AND CHILDHOOD

THIS STORY is essentially that of a phenomenal adventure in evangelism, but it is also a biography. God has willed that His work shall be done by men, and He takes infinite pains in preparing His human instruments. His preparation does not start with the birth of the individual to be used but generations before that birth. If He is to use a Moses He first puts indomitable daring into the hearts of Moses' parents. There was no accident in the matter of David's birth into the family of which Boaz and Ruth were the forebears.

And so it was with Charles Edward Fuller and Grace Payton Fuller, whom God purposed to use as leaders in a great mission to a perplexed and baffled generation. Who and what their parents were is of importance.

Mr. Fuller's father, Henry, was born in Peru, New York, in the month of January, 1846. Henrietta was his twin sister. Mother Fuller was born in Valcaur, New York, near Plattsburg, in November, 1845. Her name was Helen Maria Day. The Days were a very musical family. Four members toured that part of the country, singing and giving concerts of the highest type in many communities.

Henry and Helen Maria were married on September 10, 1867, in the old stone house which her grandfather had built. Mrs. Fuller had a fine voice and was a teacher of both voice and piano. She taught school, and above all was noted for her strong Christian character. She was of Dutch descent, large of frame and immaculate in her housekeeping. In the course of time, four sons and one daughter were born. The little daughter died in infancy.

The Fullers were Methodists. Grandfather Fuller built the old Methodist Church at Peru, New York, in 1832. Services are still held there. After the marriage of Henry and Helen Fuller, they went to Vergennes, Vermont, where Henry worked in a general store. By his thrift and hard work they were able to build a home after awhile. Later, he built and ran an excelsior factory. His health was not of the best, however, and, hearing of the beneficial southern California climate, he decided to go West. He learned that Mr. C. M. Carter, of Sierra Madre, California, was running excursions from Boston to Los Angeles and wrote to him for passage. He was invited to care for a train load of sheep being shipped to Los Angeles in exchange for his fare. Such a trip was an event of community-wide interest, in those early days, and it was with some trepidation on the part of his wife and himself that he left her and their two little boys with her mother and sister in the family home while he made the long journey. This was in the spring of 1875.

Los Angeles, at that time, was just a small town with a population of about five thousand. The streets were muddy, rutted, and lacking in beauty. There were many Mexican inhabitants in the village. But, already, a number of enterprising pioneers had settled there who were destined to become the leaders in the business life of the small but growing city.

Henry Fuller expected that his wife would join him in September, but she was thrown from a buggy by a runaway horse and seriously injured. So it was more than a year before she was recovered sufficiently to make the journey west. During this period, Father Fuller was employed in a store. After Mother Fuller's arrival, they bought a tract of land in Pomona and built a house. It was here that the baby daughter was born who later died. After some time, they returned to Los Angeles, where Father Fuller opened a furniture store. This store provided the furniture for many of the finest homes of that day. As the business grew, it was transferred to a building on Third and Main streets. This structure is still standing. During this period the family lived near the Plaza, which is now the center of the foreign population. Later they lived where the Biltmore Hotel is now located, looking out on Pershing Square, which was then a park.

Charles was born in downtown Los Angeles, at Third and Hill streets, next to the old Baptist Church, on April 25, 1887. He weighed thirteen pounds at birth. He lived in Los Angeles until he was three and a half years of age, and thereafter for several months of each year until he was seven, when his father finally disposed of all of his business in that city.

One of his earliest recollections is of being soundly spanked at the corner of Second and Spring streets. Nothing aroused his enthusiasm like a fire. At the sound of the alarm, he would dash for the truck at a near-by fire station. By the time the horses were in their places, he would be seated beside the firemen. His interest in these occasions never flagged. He particularly enjoyed the front seat of the hook and ladder truck, behind the big horses. He recalls that one day his mother, on leaving the house, told him not to go to any fires but to stay with his father at the furniture store. He would have obeyed, undoubtedly, had there been no fire, but the bell rang and off he dashed to take his place on the truck. He did not count on the proximity of his mother, however. Sitting in the street car which was passing right next to the truck, she spied the guilty Charles riding in state from the fire. Whereupon she got off the car and spanked him publicly and thoroughly.

Charles' mother was a wonderful housekeeper. She was the kind who always emptied the water out of the teakettle and turned it over on the back of the stove every night. Her home was carefully kept and she was a fine mother to her sons. Unfortunately she was, at times, afflicted with asthma. One day, in desperation, she boarded a train to get away from the city and find some relief.

She had heard that Redlands was a very healthful spot, so she investigated for herself. She stayed there for several months, taking Charles with her. Eventually she found the relief she sought.

Since the climate agreed with his wife, Father Fuller felt that he had better move to Redlands. Looking the ground over carefully in that area, he decided to settle on the southern slope of the San Bernardino Valley. He knew that where sun-flowers grew in profusion the soil must be rich. The slope he chose was yellow with sun-flowers. After disposing of his furniture store in the city, he built a big red barn and planted in oranges the seventy acres he had bought. He used certified trees of the finest stock he could procure. They soon built a three-story house with cupola and bay windows, back and front parlors, and all the appointments of a fine family residence of the Victorian period.

There were years of struggle while the grove was coming into bearing. For eight years they toiled patiently to bring it to the point of maturity. Once or twice, they almost lost it in droughts and had to drive wells hurriedly to get water. Finally they won out, and years of prosperity followed.

The grove proved to be a very profitable investment. Henry Fuller was mindful of the biblical admonition, "Bring ye all the tithes into the storehouse, that there may be meat in mine house, and prove me herewith, saith the Lord of Hosts, if I . . . will not pour you out a blessing, that there shall not be room enough to receive it," (Mal.

3:10). Eventually the grove enabled Father Fuller to be of great assistance to the missionary cause, for, with his prosperity, he was not forgetful of his responsibility to God. Not only tithes but generous gifts, as well, went to missionary work. Two trips around the world greatly increased his interest in missions, for he visited stations in many countries and saw, at first hand, their great fruitfulness. At the time of his death he was supporting, either wholly or in part, some fifty-five missionaries or native workers.

While the elder Fullers had been Christians since their childhood, they had a real, spiritual awakening about the time they moved to Redlands. Father Fuller established a large Bible class in the Methodist Church. Every week he had an exposition of the Sunday school lesson printed in the local paper, the *Redlands Daily Facts*.

Redlands was beautifully situated, overlooking a wide, fertile valley planted largely with orange trees, above which rose the snow-capped San Bernardino Mountains. The little city was settled by people of high ideals and for many years drew as residents those who were interested in Christian, as well as cultural advantages for their children. It was one of the first towns in the South to vote out the saloon.

The Fuller homestead was four miles west of Redlands, and, with the opportunity to enjoy its fine schools, churches and musical concerts, Charles grew to young manhood. People of that day lived quietly and serenely, with a trip to Los Angeles only once or twice a year.

THE FULLER HOME IN SOUTH PASADENA

"RUDY" ATWOOD AND THE QUARTETTE

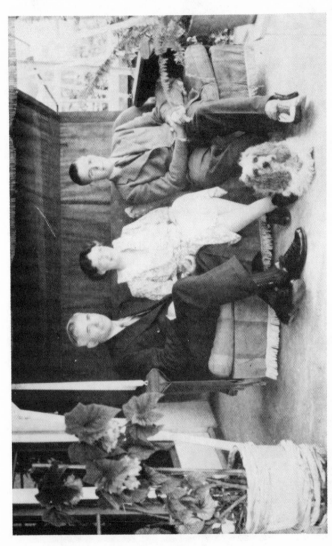

When Three Doesn't Make a Crowd

Charles hunted over the hills with his dog—and, by the way, he has always had a dog. He lived an out-of-door life. He gained in stature and physical strength as he worked on his father's ranch. He caught gophers, for which he was paid five cents each by his father. However, the nickel was not paid until the gopher tail was produced. His father wanted evidence. Charles saved enough money in this way to buy his first watch.

Every morning there was a period of family worship in the home, with Father Fuller reading from the family Bible and Mother Fuller playing a song of praise on the old Estey organ. They gathered around the organ in the evening, and sang a good deal by the light of the parlor lamp on the stand near-by.

Charles joined the church when he was about twelve years old, but in later years realized that he was not converted at that time. He made the common mistake of confusing good conduct and salvation. He rode the four miles to the high school in Redlands on his bicycle, mostly uphill. In his early high school days he was very shy. Conversation was difficult for him. He joined in few of the social activities at school but was very active in the sports, especially football. He was large for his age and had the physique and endurance to make an excellent player. At fifteen years, he was six feet tall and very broad. He wore a twelve, double E shoe.

Across the aisle from Charles, at a high school affair, sat, with her mother, a young lady—one of Charles' classmates. Both mother and daughter were greatly amused at the "twelve, double E" shoes resting on the rung of the chair in front of the fifteen year old boy; but the young lady noticed that the wearer had lovely brown eyes and she confesses now that these were what first attracted her to him.

In all, Charles played football eleven years: through grammar school, high school and college. When he finished high school there was some talk, in the family, of securing a position for him in a bank and having him start from the bottom. Mother Fuller, however, insisted on his going to college. Two older brothers had gone and she encouraged Charles to go as well. Finally Father Fuller was persuaded, although he was not entirely optimistic about his big, overgrown boy. Mother Fuller bought him his first, gray, tailored suit. He entered Pomona College, which is about thirty miles from Los Angeles, in the fall of 1906.

3

INTRODUCING ANOTHER IMPORTANT PERSON

W E MUST proceed no further until we have told another important story, that of Mrs. Charles Fuller, whose life has had a profound influence upon the ministry of her husband. Both of Grace Payton Fuller's grandparents were pioneers and came across the plains to Oregon. Her mother's father, Robert C. Kinney, came by ox-team from Iowa, in 1847, and settled with his family in Chehalem Valley, near the present site of Portland. As he started from Iowa, early one sunny spring morning, facing the unknown dangers of the immigrant trail to Oregon, his relatives remembered that, as the oxen pulled away, he was singing, "How Firm a Foundation, Ye Saints of the Lord." He was a devout Christian and, in Oregon, all the ministers who rode the circuit and the missionaries of the early days were welcomed at the Kinney home. After taking up some land, clearing it, and settling his family in a log cabin, Robert Kinney left them in the care of a brother-in-law and, in 1849, rode away to the mines in California.

Robert Kinney's wife, Elizabeth Bigelow, had come across the plains with him and their three children. She had been born in Nova Scotia and was said to be "ninety-seven pounds of ambition and courage." She bore eleven children without the assistance of a doctor. When her son Marshall, who was riding a cow, fell and came in to her with his ear hanging by a shred, the little pioneer mother threaded her needle and sewed it on, doing a very neat job. When it had healed there was only a little pucker behind the ear. Another son, Dr. Alfred Kinney, of Seaview, Washington, now eighty-six years old, remembers days when Indians were very troublesome. He recalls several nights when his mother sat by the fireplace sewing all night, not daring to go to bed, and listening to sounds of Indians outside. She would bring the children in to sleep at her feet, in the warm glow of the fire, and, sometimes, she combed little Alfred's hair with a fine comb to keep him awake, as she felt the need of company. He remembers one occasion when, with the first light of dawn creeping into the cabin, he saw his mother sitting with a gun across her knees. There was thanksgiving in her heart for the light of another day, so she sang, "Lead, Kindly Light."

By such a mother as this, and in such an environment of bravery and of Christian fortitude and trust, was reared the mother of Grace Payton Fuller.

Grace Fuller's paternal grandfather, Dr. Daniel Payton, came across the plains with his family by ox-team also, in 1849, and settled near Salem, Oregon, where he practiced medicine for many years and became dean of the first medical school in the West. Young John, who made the journey with his father and mother, when five years old, became the father of Grace Payton Fuller.

Grace was born in Drain, Oregon. Her father had followed in the footsteps of his pioneer father and become a physician. Upon John Payton's graduation from medical college, his father had advised him to start his practice of medicine in the country. He had felt that opportunities there were greater for one in general practice. Therefore, after Dr. John's marriage to Eliza Kinney in Salem, on July 4, 1874, he had taken his bride to Drain and opened up his first office there. The state normal school was located in Drain, in those days, and the town was an attractive place nestled in a valley surrounded by forest covered hills. The little church with the white spire still stands there, and also the white house of two stories, with green shutters, where Grace was born.

Dr. John's work was heavy and was made difficult because of the rainy Oregon climate. He rode to his patients on horseback, carrying drugs, bandages, and other supplies in saddle bags, often arriving drenched to the skin. On some occasions, when the need was desperate, he had to ride his swimming horse across rivers where bridges had been carried away. He loved his work in spite of all this. His first case was that of a woman who had typhoid fever. It was doubtful whether she could recover, but, giving her much personal attention and using all his skill, after two months of serious illness, she began to improve. Her husband, who was a blacksmith, said, "Well, Dr. John, I surely am thankful for what you've done for us—saving my wife's life and all. I haven't any money, but I tell you what I'll do. I'll make you a nice pair of andirons and a shovel and poker. It is the best I can do in the way of pay." Those andirons are treasured and are in use, today, in the Fuller home.

Dr. Payton was frequently paid with sheep, pigs, wheat —whatever the farmers could spare. But there must have been some payments in cash, for he managed to save enough, in a few years, to take his wife and little Grace, when the latter was four years old, to New York City, where he took a year of post-graduate work at Bellevue. His father, Dr. Daniel Payton, made the trip with them, and the two physicians, eager to learn more, frequently stayed all night at post-mortems or in the clinics. Grace can remember the apartment in which they lived, and the walks in Central Park. It was after one of these walks that the little girl was taken with diphtheria. Hers was an extremely severe case, and hope was abandoned for her recovery. But God spared her, for He had a work for her to do.

After Grace's recovery from diphtheria, in New York City, her father and mother returned with her to Drain for a short time. They then moved to Eugene, Oregon, where the State University is now located, and there her father continued to practice medicine. He was very successful in Eugene, but his little daughter was troubled with bronchitis, so it was decided that the family should move to California, where they hoped that the milder climate would benefit her. She was their only living child, as their little son had died in infancy. Naturally, their lives were wrapped up in her and her physical welfare became their great concern. They first moved to San Jose, but, hearing of the drier climate in Redlands and of the delightful community life, they located there.

Dr. Payton opened his office and began to practice medicine in Redlands in 1895. Grace was placed in school, and her health improved immediately. Throughout her school days she was well and active. Upon completion of her work in the grammar school near her home, she entered the same high school in which Charles was a student.

One day at a football game in which Charles was playing, a chum said to him, "Come on, I want to introduce you to a nice girl."

Charles, all confused and perspiring, borrowed a cap so that he might tip it when he was introduced to Grace Payton. He was very bashful, but she thought he was really nice. Though they did not become friends for some time, they never forgot that introduction, for it was the first step on the path which led to later years of great happiness together.

During high school days Grace loved fun, beautiful clothes and parties. She was a great admirer of fine and polished manners. Her parents delighted to lavish loving care upon her, and her every wish was gratified. It is a wonder she was not completely spoiled. There was a great difference between diffident Charles and other boys of her acquaintance, with their fine manners and self assurance.

During her college days there were two young men who were devoted to her. One of these was exceptionally popular with all the girls because he had a ready wit, was extremely entertaining, sang beautifully, and played the violin. Aside from this, he was strikingly handsome—"a tall blonde with violet eyes!" They had been friends for some time and, when he moved to Chicago, they corresponded regularly. So when Grace Payton wrote this young man that, on her way East to college, she and her mother and roommate would be stopping for twenty-four hours in his city, he immediately decided that he would entertain them royally. This would take money. So he set about buying and selling at a profit some used machinery then in demand. At the end of two weeks, he had a neat sum in his purse and was eagerly awaiting the arrival of the party from the West. But Grace did not even telephone this young man as she passed through Chicago, for she had looked deep into the eyes of the shy and rather quiet Charles in the last days of that summer vacation and they both realized their friendship was ripening into love.

Even in high school days she measured her acquaintances as one could wish that every young girl might do. In her heart, though not realizing it, she would wonder what sort of father each man who interested her would make. She loved little ones and hoped to mother many.

One by one, the others were found wanting as she weighed them in the balance. In spite of Charles' lack of ease, she felt in her heart that he had great stability, and that he would make the sort of father she wanted her children to have.

But we must go back a few years and watch the friendship of this young couple grow from that day when a bashful boy borrowed a cap to lift. Father Fuller had returned from a wonderful trip around the world. He came home with trunks full of curios from many lands. There were fans, ivory, ornaments, silks, oriental rugs—literally hundreds of lovely and curious things. Many of these were displayed on long tables in the parlors of the Fuller country home, and their friends in Redlands went out to see them. Their home was a popular place in those days.

It was about 1904 when, one day, two girls suggested to Grace that they hitch up the horse and drive the four miles to the Fuller ranch to see all the curios. It was warm weather and Grace took with her a fan. After several hours spent in looking over and enjoying all the interesting things, they started to leave and then realized that the fan was missing. They looked everywhere, but were unable to find it. Mother Fuller told the girls that if it were found she would send it.

The next Sunday afternoon, when the bell rang, Grace went to the door and there stood bashful Charles holding the fan—an excuse for his first visit. She invited him to come in and sit down for a few minutes. The minutes grew into hours, and then they went to the young people's meeting together. Thereafter he kept coming every Sunday. Grace attended the Baptist Church, where her father was a trustee. Charles' father was one of the leaders of the Methodist Church, and he attended there. They usually went to their respective churches in the morning, and, after taking the long drive to his ranch home for dinner, Charles hitched up the horse and drove back to Redlands to make his Sunday call. Usually he stayed for supper, and then together they went to the evening service.

Grace was very much interested in Charles' athletic ability and was a faithful attendant at the games in which he played. It was in his senior year at high school that he first asked her to marry him, but she said, "We are much too young. We both have college ahead of us. Let us not mention it again for a long time. Later on, if we find that we are suited to each other, you *might* ask me again!"

Although they were not engaged, they were together a great deal. They even managed to get a glimpse of each other on Sunday mornings fairly often, before turning in to their respective churches. Her doctor father sometimes teased her about the fellow with the large feet who was always around on Sunday. But what could Charles do? He HAD to see his girl friend, and it was much too far to drive home and then come in to church again in the evening. Surely this was sufficient excuse for staying to supper.

4

COLLEGE DAYS

Both Charles and Grace graduated from high school in the spring of 1906. That summer Grace and her parents spent in the East. The young people wrote to each other twice a week—newsy, friendly letters, and for all we know a word of love. That autumn, Charles entered Pomona College, while Grace went to Cummock School of Expression in Los Angeles. So it was, in the providence of God, that Grace Payton was being prepared for the work God had in store for her. She studied French, English, Shakespeare, history, dramatics, but especially diction and public speaking. The following year she attended Western College for Women, in Oxford, Ohio.

One amusing incident occurred during the year at Western which shows the high esteem and awe in which Mother Fuller was held as a housekeeper, and also Grace's desire for her approval. Mrs. Henry Fuller was visiting in the East and stopped off at Oxford to make a call on

Grace. When word was sent up that Mrs. Fuller was in the reception room, Grace cast an apprehensive eye over her room and, calling in a classmate to help, gave it a thorough cleaning before the guest was invited to come upstairs. So much time elapsed that Mrs. Fuller had only twenty minutes left for her visit before taking her train, but she was most gracious. Grace never admitted to her the reason for the long, long wait. Whether she knew without being told no one could say, but if she did she held her peace.

There was a fine spiritual atmosphere in Western College in those days. One of the things that impressed Grace was the "quiet time" set aside for everyone, each evening, the twenty minutes devoted to Bible study and prayer. The influence of this period was felt throughout the school. Each girl was required to give one hour of domestic service, also. Homemade bread was Grace's specialty.

After a year at Western, she returned to California for the summer and, during this time, she and Charles were together a great deal. In fact, before the summer was over they became engaged. In the fall she went to the University of Chicago.

At this time, Grace considered herself a Christian but she was not really converted. While attending the University, she went to a Unitarian Church because she so admired the minister's fine diction and liked to hear him quote Emerson and Shakespeare. She was impressed by his fine speaking voice.

Before the end of the year, her father was taken seriously ill and she was called home. He died in May, 1909. Not wishing to leave her mother to whom she was devoted, she did not finish her course in the University. Charles, however, graduated from Pomona College in the spring of 1910. He came to Redlands often during the year, as it was only about thirty-five miles by train.

Charles had developed remarkably during his college days. Always, at home, he had been the younger brother, the less colorful figure. His father had been very fond of the older boys, in whom he had seen such promise. He had given them every advantage. One of them had gone twice with him around the world. The older brother had been sent not only to college in the East, after graduating from Pomona, but to Europe also for further study. Charles had been too retiring in school, too overgrown and awkward to receive much notice from his father. He had developed something of a feeling of inferiority which persisted through his high school days. But in college he seemed to shed all this. He became a great favorite and a leader among his classmates. He was active in the dramatic club, a member of the debating team, captain of the football team, and president of his class in his senior year.

His talent for debating was not as great as his ability to advance the football toward the goal posts. He was not much of a public speaker. However, his budding ambition moved him to try everything. He remembers, even now, the climax of one of his speeches in a debate. With dramatic earnestness and emphasis he intended to say,

"Down with Anarchy," but, instead, he convulsed his audience with, "Down with Arnica." It may have ruined his climax, but a good time was had by all—except Charles. Even this, however, did not keep him from further histrionic effort.

He struggled with German and Spanish, for all languages, including English, were difficult for him. He shone in science, mathematics, history, and chemistry and graduated with a "Cum laude." In his senior year he developed height and weight until he was six feet two inches tall and weighed two hundred and ten pounds. But he worked so hard in football that during the season he went down to a mere one hundred and ninety! He loved—and still loves—football, and during his senior year, when he was captain, his team won the southern California championship. He was proficient in other sports as well—throwing the shot or discus, and in tennis. His nickname was "Chub," a tribute to his size! He was popular with the girls as well as the boys and managed to have a hand in a great deal of more or less innocent mischief.

In his senior year, Charles assisted the Professor of Chemistry. It was with money earned in this way that he bought the engagement ring for Grace, and made the trip to Oregon, where she and her mother were spending the summer, in order to present it to her. During that summer and for more than a year after finishing college, he was employed in a gold mine in northern California which was owned by his father.

This mine was in a very inaccessible place. It was of the dredger type, on the American River near Forest Hill, California. To reach it, on leaving the train, one had to ride by stage twenty miles and then walk four and a half miles down very steep, rocky grades.

This year-and-a-half period was a very lonely and rather unhappy time for the young man, just out of college. The surroundings in the mining camp were totally different from anything he had ever experienced. The week-days were full of hard labor, but on Sundays all work was suspended, by Father Fuller's orders. As he had little in common with the miners and no place to go, that one day of the week was free for reading, letter writing and thinking! Knowing him as he is today, one would have thought that Charles Fuller might have used those hours profitably in Bible study, but at that time he had no interest in spiritual things, for he had lost his faith in the infallibility of the Book by accepting the Darwinian theory of evolution in college. He was a fine, moral young man, but not interested in spiritual things, chafing under too much monotony and his dislike for the work which he was doing. His father had sent him to the mines to be overseer, but he also did the heaviest work. He heartily disliked the whole situation and stayed only because his father desired it.

One incident occurred while he was at the mine which should be recorded. Word had come to the foreman that a wall of water was sweeping down the American River, as the result of a storm at Dutch Flat, some miles above Forest Hill. Charles was asked to get into a row boat and pull himself across the river by a cable, hand over hand, and, on reaching the other side, to raise the cable by hitching it twenty feet higher. This, they hoped, would insure the safety of the dredger. Charles started, pulling as fast as he could, but when midway of the stream, the wall of water, three feet high, bore down upon him. It swept the boat out from under him, pulling him down under the water and whipping him around in a circle, first above the water, then below the surface, round and round. The men, watching from the shore, said they never expected to see him get out alive. But he managed, with almost superhuman strength, to cling to the cable and finally to pull himself to the other side, nearly drowned and completely exhausted. As he was swept under the water, he felt his time had come. His whole life passed clearly before him and he prayed, "God spare me! If you do, I'll serve you always!" He was thankful for his escape from death, but soon forgot his promise to the Lord.

In the spring of 1911, his father wrote Charles to return to Redlands and work for him in the grove. This was most agreeable to Charles, for he wanted to be near Grace. Plans were progressing for their wedding, and they were married at the home of her mother, in Redlands, on the evening of October 21, 1911.

Charles had purchased an orange grove. In an adjoining grove was an attractive house which was owned by Grace's mother. Into this the young couple moved when they returned from the wedding trip. Charles was not satisfied in working for his father on his orange groves, for he was given no opportunity to carry out any of his own ideas. He had to do each day just what he was told to do, so after a few months he secured a very good position with the Agricultural Chemical Works in Redlands.

In college he had studied chemistry and was much interested in discovering the deficiencies in soil by analysis. He could then advise a grower as to the commercial fertilizer he should use to correct these. Thus he was very successful for about a year in selling commercial fertilizer to the growers.

In 1912 there came a heavy freeze, ruining most of the fruit in that section. After this freeze, Charles installed orchard heaters in his own grove. A year later came a much harder freeze which not only ruined all the fruit but even split the bark on many of the trees around Redlands. This was a terrible blow to the citrus industry of southern California. On that memorable night in January, 1913, the growers fought a losing battle with the worst frost anyone could recall. In the later afternoon, as the thermometers were rapidly dropping, the growers began their preparations for a night of conflict. As all the men available had been hired, Mrs. Fuller dressed in her husband's clothes and worked with him all night, reading thermometers, carrying messages and helping to open the heaters, as the temperature sank lower and lower in spite of all they could do. Oranges will freeze if the temperature is at 26 degrees for two hours or more.

That night, long before midnight, with heaters wide open, the dead line had been reached, and toward morning the thermometers went as low as thirteen degrees. As the day dawned and the oil in the heaters burned low, Grace and Charles came into the house, cold and discouraged. But they looked into each other's smudgy, black faces and laughed. They had each other even though their grove was gone!

The growers had lost all of their fruit—many of the trees were gone as well. This was no time to sell fertilizer, so Charles resigned his position and decided to leave Redlands. As their own crop was gone and no funds were available for taking care of the grove, he gave that up also. They were young and full of hope, and had no fear that they could not make a new life for themselves.

5

THE CONVERSION OF THE FULLERS

OFTEN IN the background of men and women greatly used of God, it is possible to discover that some humble, unsung servant of the Lord has been used miraculously. Such was the case in the great spiritual crisis of Dwight L. Moody. Without the intercession of Mrs. Cooke and Mrs. Snow, it is doubtful if Moody would have become the greatest soul-winner of his generation. The loving providence of God was shown in a similar way in the lives of Charles and Grace Fuller. There was a humble widow, Mrs. Leonora Barnhill, who was a devout Christian and a deep student of the Word of God, whose life was happy and triumphant in spite of trying circumstances. She was used to lead Grace Payton to the Lord and, later, to influence the lives of the Fullers more than any other person. Let us go back a few years and catch a glimpse of this godly woman.

When Grace was a little girl and moved to Redlands with her parents, they lived for a short time in a rooming house where Mrs. Barnhill and her young son were residing. She had been a school teacher in the East and had come to California for her health. She was not permitted to teach without attending summer school, and this she was unable to do for lack of funds.

This gifted woman, who was so understanding and such a lover of young people, was seemingly forced to waste her talents while supporting herself and her young son by clerking in a small variety store in Redlands. She worked from eight in the morning until seven at night. Her wages were five dollars a week. Yet, even on this pitifully small stipend, she gave her tithe to the Lord and did without butter too, for years, in order to increase the amount. She lived in one room, over a corner store.

During this time, Dr. Payton was her physician, treating her for tuberculosis. On Sunday afternoons Mrs. Payton, who was kindness itself, used to take her for buggy rides and then home with her for supper. Though frail in body, Mrs. Barnhill was able to continue her work in the store until, with increased strength, she could accept a better position. She was in Dr. Payton's home from time to time, during those years, and her presence always brought sunshine and blessing. Mrs. Barnhill was a rare Christian—highly intelligent, understanding, fun-loving, and always "good company." People young and old loved to be with her, and any conversation with her turned almost invariably to spiritual things with such apparent ease that an awakened interest was kindled in the heart of the listener.

What a pity that so many Christians fail to realize the power of God's Word to transform through their witnessing, those whom they meet day by day. One does not need a college education to be a soul winner. Great preachers are not always great fruit bearers. More often those who have been truly converted can trace their conviction of sin to the moment when some humble, faithful witness for Christ brought the Word of God to bear upon their unbelief. Truly, "The Word of God is living and powerful, sharper than any two edged sword, piercing even to the dividing asunder of soul and spirit, and of the joints and marrow, and is a discerner of the thoughts and intents of the heart" (Heb. 4:12).

God proposed to use Mrs. Barnhill to win the heart of Grace Payton for Himself. Had she failed, perhaps this story could not have been written; perhaps there would have been no Old Fashioned Revival Hour.

"Though my father appreciated Mrs. Barnhill's rare worth," says Mrs. Fuller in speaking of those days, "yet he did not realize that, by ministering to her and making our home a haven for her, he was casting bread upon the waters which, after his death, would return buttered with blessings for his beloved daughter for many years to come. He was laying a foundation for a lasting friendship which greatly enriched the lives of his wife and daughter, as Mrs. Barnhill brought love, comfort, and wise counsel in times of crisis and stress and opened the eyes of his daughter to spiritual values. This was a legacy of far greater value than a deposit box full of bonds."

In further reminiscence Mrs. Fuller says, "I remember one cool evening in the summer of 1909, after my return from the University of Chicago following my father's death, when Mother, Mrs. Barnhill and I were sitting by the fireside. I was giving my Unitarian views. I said, 'You know, Barney dear, I worship only God. Christ was merely our example, our pattern for daily living.'

"Mrs. Barnhill looked at me and said, with such a loving look in her gray eyes, 'Oh, Grace, Christ said, "No man cometh unto the Father but by Me," and, my dear, you have no way of approach to a holy God unless you come through Christ, His Son, as your Saviour.'

"The Scripture which she quoted," Mrs. Fuller continues, "was the Sword of the Spirit, and at that moment Unitarianism was killed forever in my heart. I saw the light like a flash and believed at that moment, though I said nothing. She had quoted God's Word, the Spirit had used it, and, believing, I instantly became a new creation in Christ Jesus. She might have talked and even argued with me about it, but instead she just used the Word."

How many hundreds of thousands in America, today, are living outside the fold of Christ, not because of a lack of churches or preachers, but because there are no Mrs. Barnhills to speak the Word in season.

"From that time," Mrs. Fuller says, "I became interested in spiritual things. I loved to talk with Mrs. Barnhill and have her open up the Word to me. She influenced my life as she influenced every life she touched.

54

Young college people loved her, for she always seemed able to meet them on their own ground intellectually and then to lead them on to spiritual things. She exerted a great influence, later, in Charles' life."

After their marriage, the Fullers got along well financially and were taken up with the social life of their set. Mr. Fuller was not a Christian, and Mrs. Fuller was far from following the voice of God's Spirit, calling for a full surrender of her heart. "We belonged," Mrs. Fuller relates, "to a card club of young people, and we went to small dances. Oh, yes, we went to church whenever it was convenient!"

After the heavy losses in the freezes of 1912 and 1913, as we have seen, it seemed best for Charles to give up the grove on which he had been so hopefully making payments. The young couple decided to leave that section of the country, even though it would mean starting again from the beginning in a new area. Charles knew the growing of oranges, as well as the shipping and selling, from the ground up, for his father was not only a grower but a shipper, and he had worked with his father from his youth. Hearing that an orange packing house at Placentia was in need of a manager, he applied for the position. Neither Charles nor Grace had ever heard of the town before, nor did they dream of the experiences that were to be theirs while living there.

Charles went by train the fifty miles to Placentia, to interview the directors of the Mutual Packing Association. Although they felt that he was rather young, yet they must have sensed something of his ability and character at that time for, after a lengthy conference, they offered to hire him on trial for three months at a salary of one hundred dollars a month, provided he could produce good recommendations as to character. These he had no difficulty in getting from business men in Redlands. Perhaps he realized for the first time how important it is to have a good background and a character that will stand investigation.

Then came their first move. There were many to follow. They left Redlands and settled in the little town of Placentia, which was to be their home for nineteen years. After living in beautiful Redlands, Placentia looked almost impossible, for at that time it was without sidewalks or street lights. The section was rich in fine orange groves, however, and many very nice people lived there. The company for which Mr. Fuller worked was a large packing and selling organization. If he could make good he would have an excellent opportunity for advancement.

They moved into a small rented house, and Mr. Fuller immediately threw himself wholeheartedly into his work. He did so well that he was given a raise in salary within a month. Shortly thereafter they were able to purchase a home near the corner of Bradford and Chapman avenues, next to the Women's Club House. It was a tiny home with only four rooms, but attractive and comfortable. Their friends said, with amusement, that the biggest man in town lived in the smallest house! Charles Fuller is a big man. As Mr. Allen C. Emery of Boston said, many years later, on the occasion of Mr. Fuller's great meeting in Mechanics Building in that city, "He is a big man physically, a bigger man mentally, and a still bigger man spiritually." This last was not to come true for some time, but he was straightforward in his business dealings and he rapidly won the respect of his associates.

Mrs. Fuller says, of those days, "As I sat on the porch of that little house and looked across the street at an open field I never dreamed that, in a very few years, a beautiful church would stand on that corner, nor could I have imagined my husband as its pastor!"

When the Fullers moved to Placentia, Mrs. Fuller was determined that they should drop their worldly amusements and that they should cultivate the friendship of Christian people. They had many callers and were immediately invited to join a card club of the younger married set. Mrs. Fuller declined, much to her husband's disappointment, as he enjoyed playing cards and was expert, usually carrying off the prizes. He said he felt that he needed the relaxation which these games afforded. Mrs. Fuller had a deep desire to lead a separated Christian life. Mrs. Barnhill's influence was bearing fruit and, in her heart, Mrs. Fuller had a great hunger to know God in a deeper way. She wanted to attend church regularly, but Mr. Fuller preferred to spend his Sunday mornings polishing his car, reading the papers and lounging about. She often stayed away from church rather than go without him, although he sometimes went merely to please her.

Charles was always a lover of music; a taste probably inherited from his Day forebears. In Placentia, an old fashioned singing society, called the Philharmonic, had flourished for thirty years. The Fullers were asked to join. They did; and they greatly enjoyed the meetings which were held in different homes, when everyone sang lustily. Mr. Fuller later sang bass in the Orpheus Club in Los Angeles.

Thus was the Lord preparing him even along musical lines for the supervision of the Old Fashioned Revival Hour; for music has always been an important part of that ministry from the beginning. In no small measure has the singing of the old gospel hymns contributed to the spiritual success of this Hour, not only because of the spirit in which they are sung but because of the fine quality of the music itself.

During the early years in Placentia, Charles took a correspondence course in accounting and business methods. He enjoyed this greatly, studying far into the night. Doubtless God put it into his heart to do this as part of the training for the future work which He had for him to do.

Mrs. Barnhill was a frequent visitor in the little home in Placentia, during those years, and many hours were spent in Bible study. When she was with them, she and Grace attended Dr. Johnson's Bible class in Anaheim, four miles away. Mr. Fuller would take his wife, who went regularly on Tuesday evenings, but he would not go himself. While she was at the class, he would attend a picture show and then pick her up afterward. She soon became very deeply interested in these Bible studies and purchased a Scofield Reference Bible for the benefit of its helpful notes.

On one of Mrs. Barnhill's visits she had with her a book of biblical prophecy, entitled, "Mysteries of the Kingdom," which Grace read. It gripped her heart, as she looked up the references in the Bible. One day she cornered Charles and said, "Oh, my dear, I want you to read this book! It is simply thrilling how God has dealt with Israel through the years, and what is to come to pass in His plan!"

For the first time she was able to arouse his interest, and he read the book through. From that time his attitude toward spiritual things began to change.

After living in Placentia for about a year, Charles and Grace were happy in looking forward to the arrival of a little one in their home. Great was their disappointment and sorrow when they lost that baby. Soon after this, Grace developed tuberculosis and was obliged to give up all active duties for about five years, living on the screened porch of their little home. She went to the mountains during the summer heat, and it was while she was absent, one of these summers, that Charles was converted.

In these modern times, unfortunately, there is a constant effort to get away from the old phraseology used by Christians in other days. *Conversion* is discarded for *Change*. An attempt at revival becomes a *Crusade*, or a *Preaching Mission*. *Sin* is sanctified by calling it an *error*

of judgment, or a *stumble in the upward path to God.*
Oh, that God would raise up a new generation of evange-
lists in these terrifying times of wickedness, hatred and
apostasy to preach the truth without compromise, as did
Jonathan Edwards, Charles Finney, Dwight L. Moody,
and Billy Sunday! These have passed off the field of
action, going to their abundant reward, and who is to take
up the banner which they are no longer here to carry?

Fortunately, at this time of crisis in the life of Charles
Fuller, he did not chance upon a "pink tea" type of revival service. He had the good fortune to be led where
he would hear God's Word preached by one who had all
the fervor of a Whitfield.

One Saturday, as he read the newspaper, Mr. Fuller
noticed that a man whom he had known in college days
as an amateur wrestler and boxer was going to preach the
next day in Los Angeles. He could hardly believe his
eyes, because when he knew him this man had seemed far
removed from spiritual things. He determined to go into
the city, the next day, and hear him. Taking a seat far
back in the auditorium, partly hidden behind a column,
Charles Fuller listened intently, drinking in every word
as this man of God spoke from Ephesians. The text of
his sermon was, "The eyes of your understanding being
enlightened that you may know what is the hope of his
calling and what the riches of the glory of his inheritance
in the saints" (Eph. 1:18).

As he listened he became deeply convicted. He had
entered that auditorium a self-satisfied young man, feel-

ing no need of God, but as he listened he saw himself as a sinner in need of a Saviour. As the speaker continued with his sermon, using much Scripture, the Holy Spirit used the Word to melt Charles' heart, and he dropped his head on the seat in front of him. He did not understand his own feelings, but there came to him a vision of Christ as his Saviour, and he felt the call of God to yield to Him and to give his life for His service.

A tremendous struggle went on in his heart, as the Sword of the Spirit pierced deeply. Leaving the auditorium at the end of the service, he got into his car, deep in thought, and drove out to Hollywood to a quiet spot at the edge of Franklin Park. He felt that he wanted to get away by himself and think. Stopping under some eucalyptus trees, late that Sunday afternoon in July, he got down on his knees in the back of the car and there, after a long struggle, finally yielded to God.

Hollywood may be the most famous city in the world as the rendezvous of theatrical talent—a place where shopgirls, clerks, stenographers and cowboys are transformed into glamorous stars; where money flows like water and where sinful pleasures are made to seem respectable. But, to Charles Fuller, Hollywood means far more than any of these relatively insignificant things. For him, the shadow of those eucalyptus trees is the temple of God, a Bethel! For him, it is the place of his spiritual birth. For the first time he really breathed the breath of Life. On that wonderful day, Hollywood became the place where the morning stars again sang together and the orchestra of

Heaven broadcast the news that a new witness to the saving and cleansing power of the blood of Christ had been commissioned. It was, for him, the unlocking of a vast storehouse of wealth in God, more enriching than the contents of all the banks of California. He flew over the treetops—no, not really, but it seemed that way. Returning to the auditorium that evening, to hear the same speaker, his heart was filled with joy unspeakable, and he felt himself truly a new creation in Christ Jesus. Old things had passed away, and all things had become new.

Is it not significant that in Hollywood should occur, after many years, the first broadcast of the Old Fashioned Revival Hour? It was from the Woman's Club in that city that the first major hook-up was sent forth, eighteen years later. But you will hear more of that in due time.

6

EARLY MINISTRY

Mrs. Fuller's joy was great when she received word from her husband of the great change which had come into his life. He told her that all his former ambitions for making money and for worldly success were gone, and that now his whole desire was to be of service to God. She says, "I realized when I read the letter that there had been an 'about face,' and I wondered where we should be led out in service to God. Should we be called to the mission field? I wondered if I could be a good missionary! I hoped we should not be called to a hot country. I was conscious that the whole trend of our lives would be changed from then on, and I was willing to go wherever God called my husband, and help as much as I could."

After making his momentous decision on that July afternoon, Mr. Fuller returned to Placentia and began right away to study the Bible diligently. Not only that, but he started a Bible class at once, although he knew very little about the Book in spite of the fact that he had grown up in a Christian home.

Mrs. Fuller relates some of his early efforts. "Soon after his conversion I remember, one rainy afternoon, that he sat down by the fireplace with his feet on the mantle and said he was going to begin by learning the books of the Bible."

His first attempt at teaching his newly formed Bible class was in the book of Daniel. He had Dr. Gaebelein's book on the subject and kept just a chapter ahead of the class. The class was held in the Presbyterian Church in Placentia and had a most unusual name. It was called, "The Unearthly Hour Bible Class," for it was held at eight o'clock in the morning each Sunday. Many members of the class were teachers in Sunday schools and had to be in their places by half past nine. From the beginning, this class studied with enthusiasm and grew rapidly in numbers, as the studies in prophecy were new to most of them.

After this early morning class, the Fullers would drive to Los Angeles to listen to Dr. R. A. Torrey, who was then Dean of the Bible Institute. His incomparable teaching was deeply appreciated and was a great blessing in developing the Fullers' understanding of the Scriptures. But they were embarrassed to have the people of Placentia know that they were going out of town. They would try to slip out quietly, but their collie dog, "Captain," delighted at the prospect of a trip, would bark all the way out of town, advertising to the whole community that the Fullers were on their way to Los Angeles.

As we may well imagine, Mrs. Barnhill was happy over Charles' conversion. Talking with her about spiritual things was always a delight, and as she drew from her own rich experience in conversation she exerted a great influence upon Charles' thinking.

The truth of the Lord's return has always been very dear to Mr. Fuller since he first began to study the Bible. And it has given to him a sense of urgency. He feels he must do his utmost to win as many souls to Christ as possible before He comes.

As his Bible class in Placentia grew it became necessary to find a new meeting place. The Woman's Club House was procured. Many of the members were married and had small children whom they brought with them to the class. There was a growing desire for a Sunday school, and soon one was organized. So the work grew and prospered.

After Mr. Fuller's conversion, he continued in his position as manager of the Fruit Association, where he was successful and highly regarded. But God was calling him to surrender all to Him—to put the future in His hands and to walk the paths into which He would lead. Charles heard God speaking to him and he answered, "Yes, Lord, I do want to be used by Thee. I am teaching a Bible class. I am studying the Bible. Can I not keep my position and work for Thee still? Anyway, you know I NEVER could preach!"

Months passed in which every spare hour was spent in Bible study. So thirsty was he for knowledge of the Book that he ceased to read magazines and books which he previously had enjoyed, and he scarcely looked at a newspaper. He found great joy in Bible study, and God became increasingly real and dear to him.

One day, as Charles sat at the desk in his business office, he could not keep his mind on the matters before him. The work he was doing seemed futile in the light of eternity. Again he felt God speaking to him, calling him to leave his position and step out in faith in full time service. Two years before, Charles had purchased an orange grove on which he had made several payments. He kept turning over in his mind the problem of how he could care for his wife and keep up the payments on this grove if he left his work. How could he finance three years of training for Christian work? And, moreover—the greatest question—HOW COULD HE EVER PREACH! He had no gift for public speaking, no fluency. There were other things he could do well, but surely God would not ask him to PREACH.

He was so disturbed in mind and heart that he arose, went down the stairs, through the packing house where men and women were working, back to the storage room where great piles of shook (lumber of which orange boxes are made) were stored. There he knelt behind a pile of shook, as God dealt with him. It was a long struggle, for Satan kept telling Charles Fuller how foolish he would be to give up his position, to throw to the winds all his opportunities for advancement, to lose the grove, probably, on which he had paid everything he had. Further, Satan pictured to him what a fizzle he would be as a preacher. "Now, if you had talent and a large vocabulary—if you could preach fine, flowery sermons, it would be different. But YOU—you would be a joke as a preacher!"

Charles arose and started to go out, only to turn back and fling himself down in the sawdust, praying, "Oh, Lord, I will walk in your path. I will do what you want me to do. I will even try to preach, if you can use me. I will resign my position and trust you to supply our needs. I want to be used in saving souls, for that is all that really counts in this world."

After telling Grace of his decision, they both began to pray that God would direct them and provide for their needs, if He wanted Charles to take training for Christian work. Within three weeks an official of an oil company came to see if he might lease their land with the privilege of sinking oil wells there. Large oil fields had been developed near Placentia. In looking for new oil developments, the geologists had become convinced that the Fuller grove was near the western end of the dome. For the privilege of sinking wells on this land Charles was offered a check for ten thousand dollars! Strange to say, no oil well was ever placed on that land, but this money enabled Charles to meet payments on the grove, to care for it, and to provide for three years of training for Christian service. What a wonderful God we have!

When he handed in his resignation, the Board of Directors were reluctant to accept it. They could not understand why he should wish to leave a fine business opportunity to go into religious work. One member of the Board who was a close friend of Charles said to him, "Well, I hate to see you make this change. I think it is a mistake. You are too good a man for the ministry."

How characteristic of the wisdom of the world is this statement. How difficult it is for men to see that there can be no business or professional position comparable to that of bringing lost men out of eternal Death into eternal Life, through the acceptance of Jesus Christ as their Lord and Saviour. These years of executive training in the business world proved to be a necessary part of his preparation for the unique ministry which God had in His plan for him. Had he continued in the business world and been successful, he would have been known only to a comparatively small circle, and his life would have been, in all probability, fruitless in the light of eternity. As in the case of Abraham, obedience had to come before blessing. By taking the way of the cross, a way which seemed but foolishness to his associates, Charles Fuller has proved the truth of the Scripture, "Except a corn of wheat fall into the ground and die it remains what it was, a single grain. But if it die, it yields a rich harvest." Because he was willing to die to all his worldly ambitions, doing what seemed impractical, even to himself, he has since been a blessing to countless millions.

In spite of urgent dissuasion of friends and associates,

he remained firm in his decision to resign from his position. He entered the Bible Institute of Los Angeles in September, 1919, and graduated in 1921. He returned for another year of special study in doctrine under Dr. Torrey. Mrs. Fuller was with him for a year at the Institute, but thereafter stayed in Placentia to supervise the care of the grove. Charles went back and forth daily on the train.

During the three years of his study at the Institute, the Bible class continued to thrive in Placentia. Charles had been considering service on the mission field and was looking to God for leading in that direction. But the members of the Bible class, which was outgrowing the Women's Club, were eager to found an interdenominational church. After much prayer and many conferences it seemed to be God's leading that they should do this, and the money was forthcoming from those interested to build a very nice church in Placentia, at the corner of Bradford and Chapman avenues. This building was dedicated in February, 1926, as Calvary Church. Mr. Fuller had been ordained as a Baptist minister on May 4, 1925. Upon the completion of the church, he became its pastor.

For years the Fullers had greatly desired a little one to gladden their home in place of the babe who had fallen asleep. They had been married twelve years and had no children. Mrs. Fuller's health had improved, though she was still far from strong. However, the Lord graciously granted their desire, and a son was born to them on August 28, 1925, whom they named Daniel Payton.

At times, during this period before Daniel's birth, Mrs. Fuller's strength was a matter of grave concern. God gave her wonderful comfort from His Word, many times. Once, when there was great apprehension and special need, on January 13, 1925, she opened her little book, Daily Light, and read: "Thou wilt keep him in perfect peace, whose mind is stayed on thee. Cast thy burden upon the Lord, and he shall sustain thee. I will trust and not be afraid; for the Lord Jehovah is my strength and song; He also is become my salvation. In quietness and in confidence shall be your strength. The effect of righteousness (shall be) quietness and assurance forever. . . ." At the bottom of the page, Mrs. Fuller made the following notation, on that day. "In nausea, in fear, in weakness, what a comfort! I will trust and NOT BE AFRAID! How precious!" And on these wonderful promises she stayed her heart during those difficult days.

The coming of little Danny into the home made their cup full to overflowing. God had shown His goodness and mercy to them in so many ways. Their financial need had been miraculously met during the days of preparation for the gospel ministry; a little one had come to bless their home, and now Charles was finding great joy in his ministry for God at Calvary Church. Though he still felt he could not preach, yet he could teach the Bible. He continued to study God's Word diligently, and as he gave it out to the people he found it acceptable to his congregation.

The village of Placentia had now grown to a sizable

town of about three thousand inhabitants, and this fundamental church was becoming a place of real spiritual power in the country round about. Mr. Fuller brought to the church the finest of conference speakers and missionary leaders from all parts of the world. He himself engaged, and paid the salaries of two trained workers, one for boys and one for girls. Altogether, there were twelve clubs for Bible study for boys or girls held in the church weekly. It was often called a young people's church. The spirit of revival was present in a remarkable way, and a full program was carried on twelve months of the year.

Mr. Fuller's pastorate extended from 1925 until 1932. During that time he drew no salary from the church, but supported himself from his orange groves and other business enterprises. He was able not only to care for his own family but to help in a very substantial way in providing for the financial need of the church. Like Paul, he found joy in preaching the gospel without charge while he "made tents" for a living. With the many spiritual activities of the church and the demands of his business, he was more than busy day and night—happy in the service of the Lord.

DARK DAYS

T HEN CAME the crash of 1929. Real estate values dropped; bank loans were called; crops glutted the market; unemployed men and women filled the streets of the cities. Over-expansion found a great majority of the business men of America unprepared, and, in the providence of God, Charles Fuller was caught with the rest. He might have saved himself much distress but for his anxiety to help those who were dependent upon him. He made every effort to carry his employees during this period of stress and unemployment.

He, in common with most business men, expected that the panic would be of brief duration and that, with the return of normal conditions, loans could be repaid from the sale of his crops. But things did not work out as expected and before he could let go of his groves he was carried more deeply into debt. At that time he owned two hundred and fifty acres of orange land in the heart of one of the most productive areas of California. No one could truthfully say that he had continued business from any selfish motive after that day in the packing house when he had, with such a struggle, fully consecrated his life to the service of God. His interest in business continued solely that he might be self-supporting and give to the cause of Christ. His whole ambition was that his business might contribute to the propagation of the gospel.

But God had a higher plan for him than this. There was constant danger that the time devoted to business would hinder his ministry. In addition to his duties in his church he was on several missionary boards and was President of the Board of Trustees of the Bible Institute of Los Angeles. The Institute was feeling the effect of the business depression, and he was having to give much time and thought to its affairs.

During these dark days his creditors were pressing him severely; some of them were threatening to throw him into bankruptcy. This he was determined to avoid, if possible, feeling a deep concern that God should not be dishonored by his failure to meet his obligations. As time went on, he was fighting more and more with his back to the wall, pleading with his creditors to give him a little time, hoping that he might dispose of some properties and thus meet his obligations. All he asked was time to make some sales and get a little money from his orange crops that he might be able to make payments when obligations fell due. Day after day he was in conference with various business men and his attorney in

Los Angeles in an effort to find a way out. Sometimes things looked utterly hopeless, as though at any time he might be thrown into involuntary bankruptcy—but still he fought on.

It would be useless to attempt to explain why God allowed His servants to be caught in the financial debacle which brought ruin to so many thousands of the most astute business men. It is, of course, easy to say, as many did, that if Charles had obeyed the Lord he and his wife would have been spared the sorrow and anxiety of those years. Perhaps that is so. There may have been unconscious failure; there may have been too great a degree of self-reliance born of years of business success; perhaps uninterrupted prosperity would have led Charles to neglect his high calling as a minister of Christ.

This much is sure. Charles and Grace Fuller were lovers of God. Therefore, they could claim the promise that "all things work together for good to them that love God, to those who are the called according to His purpose" (Romans 8:28). The refining process through which they were to pass, for a period of five years, was to make them more fit than they otherwise could possibly have been for the task of "preaching the gospel to the poor, healing the broken-hearted, preaching deliverance to the captives, and the recovering of sight to the blind, setting at liberty them that are bruised and preaching the acceptable year of the Lord," as did their Master. How could they have understood the hearts of the thousands of defeated men and women who were to turn to them for the Word of Life if they had not tasted the cup of sorrow themselves?

While Mr. Fuller was out fighting his financial battle on many fronts, his wife and little Mrs. Barnhill, and oftentimes Major Osborn, too, would be at home praying that God would undertake for him and show him the way through. Major Osborn was an Anglican clergyman visiting in the United States, a deeply spiritual friend and prayer warrior. He was a tower of strength to the Fullers at this time of testing.

Many times they went to Daily Light for comfort. The following are some of the verses of Scripture which God gave them: On July 27, 1934, at a time when Charles was fighting through a particularly difficult situation, they read, "Thou hast girded me with strength unto the battle. When I am weak, then am I strong. Asa cried unto the Lord his God, and said, 'Lord, it is nothing with Thee to help, whether with many, or with them that have no power; help us, O Lord our God; *for we rest on Thee,* and in Thy name we go against this multitude. O Lord, Thou art our God; let not man prevail against Thee.' Jehoshaphat cried out, and the Lord helped him. It is better to trust in the Lord than to put confidence in man."

"For we rest on thee" was a direct message, because they were so weary in the battle. He gave them His rest.

At another time of discouragement and distress, in business matters, they turned to Daily Light, on September 2nd, and again God spoke comfort, as follows: "Wait on the Lord: be of good courage, and He shall strengthen thy heart. Hast thou not known? Hast thou not heard that the everlasting God, the Lord, the creator of the ends of the earth, fainteth not, neither is weary? . . . He giveth power to the faint; and to them that have no might He increaseth strength. Fear thou not, for I am with thee: be not dismayed, for I am thy God; I will strengthen thee; yea, I will help thee; yea, I will uphold thee with the right hand of my righteousness. The trying of your faith worketh patience. But let patience have her perfect work, that ye may be perfect and entire, wanting nothing. Cast not away, therefore, your confidence, which hath great recompence of reward. For ye have need of patience, that, after ye have done the will of God, ye might receive the promises."

Mrs. Fuller has marked this, in the margin; "What comfort in our extremity.—Isn't this wonderful!"

In the midst of all these difficulties came illness, and it was necessary for Mrs. Fuller to undergo a major operation. Funds were very low, but the need was supplied, and they gave thanks to their heavenly Father. Then came the serious illness of Danny. He had been a very healthy, happy baby, and the rare enjoyment of watching him develop into a sturdy child was turned into anxiety. When he was four and a half years old he contracted whooping cough. His was a severe case and before he had recovered from that he developed pneumonia. The next winter he took pneumonia again, and was desperately ill.

One never to be forgotten morning during this illness, when Charles was meeting financial difficulties which seemed beyond any human solution, he left early to go to an attorney's office in Los Angeles. As usual, he and his wife prayed before he left, asking for wisdom and the guidance of God. Danny was worse, that morning, because of coughing. A fine Christian nurse, Josephine Sundstrom, was with Mrs. Fuller. To many of her friends she was just "Sunny." She was a great comfort to the Fullers for, aside from being an excellent nurse, she knew how to pray and was always ready to help them when they needed her.

On this particular morning the doctor had suggested that if Dan could be turned over on his chest, the mucus, which was so difficult to cough up, might be gotten rid of more quickly. So the thin little body was turned. The coughing increased and, as he caught his breath, part of the mucus was drawn into a bronchial tube. This caused greatly increased coughing, as nature seemed to be trying to expel the particle. As the little fellow choked, he grew weaker and weaker. "Sunny," realizing the seriousness of the situation, called the doctor but could not reach him. She called another from a nearby town, urging him to come at once. In the meantime, she called the fire department to bring an oxygen tank. This they used on the fast weakening child.

When the doctor arrived, he could find no pulse in the little wrist. He gave a heart stimulant and asked whether they had some ether and olive oil. How thankful Mrs.

Fuller was to be able to bring these immediately. He mixed them and gave them to Dan as an enema. As soon as the ether was absorbed, the coughing ceased and Dan lay quiet, the color of ashes, his breath coming in fluttering little gasps. The doctor said he had just read of this treatment in a medical journal but had never tried it before. He was pleased with the result, although he warned Mrs. Fuller that in time the effects of the ether would wear off and nature would again try to expel the particle by coughing. He feared that in his weakened condition Danny could not endure more coughing and suggested that he be taken in an ambulance to Los Angeles, where a bronchoscope might be used in removing the particle. He warned them that the trip might prove dangerous because of the congestion in the lungs, and that such a long journey would be tiring to the heart.

The decision as to what would be best to do would have to be made by Mrs. Fuller and the nurse, for the doctor felt reluctant to advise them which course to follow. After prayerful consideration, it was finally decided to take Danny the twenty-eight miles to the city, and preparations were made for the trip. Constant prayer was going up to God that, if it were His will, the little life might be spared.

Meanwhile, Mr. Fuller in the attorney's office was called to the telephone and informed that he had better come home quickly as Danny was dangerously ill and oxygen was being used in an effort to save his life. He rushed to the elevator and, as he went down, his knees almost went out from under him. With a rebellious heart he got into his automobile and started for home. He drove too rapidly for safety through the traffic, and as he went he prayed, "Oh, Lord, I have tried to serve you but if you take our little boy I'm THROUGH! This is one thing I just can't endure, Lord. I can't give him up. I can't go on if you take him."

He drove on mile after mile and gradually the rebellion in his heart melted and he said, "Yes, Lord, Thy ways are best—I yield to Thee and want Thy will done." And he found himself singing that sweet old song:

> "I will say, 'Yes,' to Jesus,
> 'Yes, Lord, forever yes':
> I'll welcome all Thy blessed will,
> And sweetly answer, 'Yes.' "

When he reached home he hurried into the nursery where Danny lay unconscious in his little bed, breathing irregularly. He was bluish in color, with great circles under his eyes. Mr. Fuller leaned over him and, after taking one long, loving look, knelt by the bed, saying, "This is a time for prayer." Mrs. Fuller, in telling of the incident, says, "Never shall I forget that scene and that prayer! On Mr. Fuller's uplifted face I saw mingled grief and sweet surrender, and never have I heard such a touching prayer. He said, 'I thank you, Lord, for these five and a half years that we have had this little boy. He has been such a blessing in our home. We shall miss him so, but take him to yourself, if that is your will. "The

Lord has given and the Lord has taken away. Blessed be the name of the Lord." We are giving him back to you, our Father.' Then he arose from his knees, trusting the Lord whatever might be the outcome."

The ambulance drove up to the door and little Danny, wrapped in blankets, with his head and ears covered by his red stocking cap, was carried out. "Sunny" and Mrs. Fuller sat beside him, balancing on the slippery seats as they went around the corners at a rapid pace. The doctor and Mr. Fuller followed in another car with an oxygen tank. They were praying earnestly that God might spare the little boy, if it were His will, and that the trip would not prove injurious. As consciousness began to return and the brown eyes opened, Mrs. Fuller read to Dan to keep him quiet, though she knew not a word that she read, holding his thin little hand in her own.

When they arrived in Los Angeles, it was dusk. Kind nurses had remained after closing hours. The rooms were all warm and brightly lighted. Little Dan was carried in and placed on the table for examination. The fluroscope showed NO SIGN OF A PLUGGING PARTICLE! The doctor said, "There is no need to use the bronchoscope. The plug has apparently been absorbed, but the pneumonia is general throughout his lungs, so do not expect too much. If he has a very strong heart he may survive."

Dan looked up into his mother's face and said, "Mother, I'm hungry." So he was given a little gelatin, then carried back in the ambulance to Placentia. He began a slow

The Chorus Choir of the Old Fashioned Revival Hour

THE BROADCAST

recovery from that day. How doubly precious he became, and how thankful were Charles and Grace Fuller that God had spared him to them. It was six years before he fully regained his health and strength, but today he is a fine, strong boy, taller than his mother, interested in his hobbies and sports, and a great joy to his parents.

Along with severe financial trials and the still more heartbreaking ordeal of the illness of Mrs. Fuller and Dan, came the additional testing of misunderstanding, and the desertion of some of Mr. Fuller's closest friends. Among Job's sorest afflictions were the taunts and criticisms of his supposed comforters, and there were not wanting those who pointed an accusing finger at Charles Fuller in the midst of his distress, saying that he must be under the displeasure of God to be visited with such reverses. There had been no lack of friends when all was going well. But now that the hand of God seemed heavy upon him, even some of the brethren in the church which he had done so much to establish and maintain turned away from him.

It would be difficult for anyone who had not passed through the same distressing experience to understand how those who had been the recipients, on many occasions, of his generosity, could fail to sympathize with him in the time of his trial. Both Mr. and Mrs. Fuller were cut to the heart with these experiences, but God was permitting them for their further spiritual enrichment, thus giving them a post-graduate course in order that they might be fit to minister to the millions who experience so many kinds of heartbreak. Moses, also, went to God's school of adversity, where for forty years in the depths of a wilderness he suffered exile from those he loved and longed to deliver from bondage, whose misunderstanding of his purpose had been part of *his* postgraduate course in suffering.

The strain of all of this was telling upon Mr. Fuller physically. Night after night he spent sleepless hours, and when he did fall asleep for a short period he sighed and tossed, with rest broken. Mrs. Fuller would reach out for his hand and quote Scripture to him for his comfort, and together they would call upon God to sustain them and to deliver them in His own good time. Mr. Fuller had been a man of unusual strength and physical health, but his weight fell from two hundred forty pounds to one hundred ninety. He became very pale, and dark circles appeared under his eyes. Sometimes he preached in Calvary Church when the fatigue as a result of the strain was so great that he could scarcely stand long enough to complete his message.

Again and again, when the burdens were heavy, they would go to God in prayer and there find comfort and release. The verse which became most precious to them in those days was Psalm 37:5: "Commit thy way unto the Lord, trust also in Him and He shall bring it to pass."

Frequently, they would pick up a book and say, "Now, Father, this represents our problem," and laying it down would continue, "We place it in Thy hands, asking Thee to work it out for Thy glory and for our good. Now that we have committed it, help us to really trust Thee, for Thou hast promised that when we commit and trust Thou wilt work. We thank Thee that Thou art working out a solution for this problem right now."

Their constant prayer was, "Lord, help us to trust." And during those darkest days, God was very real. He comforted their hearts, giving them the peace that passeth understanding. On numberless occasions, when they felt they could go no further, God would encourage them with answers to prayer and their hearts would rejoice with thanksgiving to Him.

Mrs. Fuller testifies, "Never once did God fail us! In all this, He was bringing us to the place where we were willing to say, "Yes, Lord, take everything. Do anything, but let Charles continue in Thy ministry, for Thy glory."

Another chapter was being completed in the life of the man God purposed to greatly use. With grief of heart, still not realizing the greatness of God's plan for him, he placed his resignation in the hands of the trustees of Calvary Church and moved from Placentia.

8

BROADCASTING THE GOSPEL

WHILE ATTENDING a Bible conference in Indianapolis, in 1927, Mr. Fuller was invited to "pinch hit" on a gospel radio program in place of the regular speaker. Always glad of an opportunity to witness for his Lord, he agreed to fill in the fifteen minutes. This was his first experience before a microphone. He had always thought it would be a difficult thing to forget the little instrument into which one must speak when broadcasting and that he would feel constrained and limited. But there was a message burning in his heart and he was determined to do his best to put it across.

He prepared carefully and when he finally stood before the microphone all hesitancy and fear left him. He forgot the microphone and, closing his eyes, spoke earnestly to the listening, unseen audience. This has been his way of speaking ever since and is one of the reasons for his great success in this field, quite different from a pulpit ministry. He says that in speaking before the microphone he is unconscious of it or anyone around him and has in mind some lonely miner or bedridden person to whom he speaks.

That morning in Indianapolis, his message was taken from Mark 4:35–41, where the account is given of our Lord stilling the storm for His disciples on the Sea of Galilee. He called attention to four things in his text: A Great Peril, A Great Plea, A Great Peace, and A Great Personage.

He was somewhat disturbed, the next day, when the regular speaker on that program asked him what he had said over the radio the day before. With some embarrassment, he replied that he had given a simple gospel message and inquired if there had been any complaints because of it. "Oh, no," replied the other, "but we've had so many letters telling of the blessings received from your message that I wondered just what it was about."

Three nights later, while sleeping on the train from Philadelphia to Chicago, God awoke him and gave him a vision of the possibilities of sending out the gospel *by radio*. He laid on his heart such an overwhelming burden of prayer that he could hardly endure it. He was given an assurance that radios would become increasingly popular until nearly everyone would own one. The tremendous, almost unbelievable possibilities of reaching the lost by means of this comparatively new invention were borne in upon him so forceably that, for several hours, he cried out to God in prayer that God would work mightily for the spread of the gospel over the whole land by this means. He knew only God could bring this to pass. After several hours, the burden was lifted and he felt that God had heard. Finally he slept once more.

With a growing conviction that radio would be a wonderful means of spreading the gospel and of reaching people wherever they might be, he arranged, in February, 1928, for a series of broadcasts from Calvary Church at Placentia, of which he was pastor at the time. The morning and evening church services were broadcast. Later he added a Thursday evening Bible class. This latter proved to be a great spiritual blessing and Mr. Fuller is still hearing of those who were converted while listening to that hour. These broadcasts from Calvary Church, over KGER, Long Beach, continued until March, 1933, when Mr. Fuller resigned from Calvary Church.

Feeling led to give his time entirely to the broadcasting of the gospel, he arranged for a Sunday morning and evening hour to be released from the studio of KGER, in Long Beach. There could scarcely have been a worse time, from the standpoint of human reasoning, to attempt anything requiring financial expenditure. On March 10, 1933, came the big earthquake. On March 13, every bank in the country was closed. But in spite of discouraging conditions, Charles Fuller was confident that God had spoken and he courageously continued with his plans for broadcasting over the Long Beach station. His own property was gone and he was entirely dependent on the offerings of his listeners for the money with which to pay for the broadcast. God so wonderfully provided funds that first week of the bank holiday, when in all human expectation not a cent would come in, that he had sufficient money not only to pay for his broadcasts for the week but even to lend a few dollars to some millionaire acquaintances who found themselves caught without cash and knew no bank was open from which to draw.

Right after the earthquake the city was under martial law and it was with great difficulty that he procured permission to get to the broadcasting studio.

During these early days of broadcasting, Mrs. Fuller was with Danny on the desert, where they had taken him that he might recover from his illness in the dry air. Mr. Fuller made every effort to join them on Sunday nights, taking the long drive out after the evening service and usually arriving sometime after midnight. They were still under great financial stress, and it seemed that God, in His goodness, had provided this desert retreat in order that His servant might have a few hours of quiet prayer and refreshment each week, beyond the reach of the telephone. Mrs. Fuller cooked tempting dishes for her husband and surrounded him with love and cheer. Together they revelled in watching Danny's return to rosy good health. Both Charles and Grace look back upon those days in Miss White's cottage in the village of Palm Springs as among the happiest of their lives.

During this time Mr. Fuller was broadcasting the "Pilgrim Hour" from the Long Beach studio, from 11:00 to 12:00 each Sunday. People began to drop in to enjoy the broadcast. The numbers grew until there were about three hundred coming regularly.

The "Pilgrim Hour" continues to the present time, and the same group is standing by as Mr. Fuller's "prayer warriors." To this faithful company the Fullers attribute the large ministry of these later years. Although there is no church organization, yet this group is banded together in love and is like a small church. Whenever there are special problems it is to these friends that Mr. Fuller goes for assistance in intercession. Each month they have a communion service together. The messages are on the deeper Bible truths, given for the feeding of the flock of God. Mr. Fuller revels in thus opening up the Word to believers there in the studio, as well as over the air, each Sunday morning. He himself derives real spiritual blessing in preparation for this weekly broadcast. It keeps him fresh and on tiptoe spiritually, for his evening messages given on the Old Fashioned Revival Hour are necessarily very simple, and largely to the unsaved.

When the Fullers gave up their church in Placentia, they first moved to Fullerton and then to San Marino, which is a suburb of Los Angeles. They hoped the drier air near the mountains would be beneficial to Danny, and it was.

The years in San Marino were very happy ones, though they were far from easy. In fact, some of their greatest trials and testings came to them there. But, again, they found that as they faced them, resting on Psalm 37:5, God's presence was very real. His answers to prayer were so definite that their days were really joyful. The home where they then lived has become to them a sacred spot. They like to drive past it today because of its precious associations. Trials, sorrow, bitter waters, yes—but peace was there too, because of the Everlasting Arms on which they leaned.

Mr. Fuller was still fighting his financial battle. Many times Mrs. Fuller, Dr. Tom (Osborn) and, of course, dear little Mrs. Barnhill met in the living room of the San Marino home to engage in earnest intercession while Mr. Fuller was in the city. It was during these days that a trusted partner went into bankruptcy, leaving heavy obligations for Mr. Fuller to meet. These were not morally his and it seemed most probable, from a human standpoint, that he would not be able to weather the storm if he assumed responsibility for them. But God wonderfully undertook, time after time, until victory finally came and the crisis was successfully passed.

In the spring of 1935, Mr. Fuller had sixty names on his mailing list—friends who were supporting the work by offerings or prayer, or both. He was having a most difficult time carrying on, yet the work was fruitful and God's hand was undoubtedly upon it. While praying for wisdom to meet the problems he faced, he felt led to write a letter to each of these friends telling them something of the vision he had for reaching people by radio "right where they are," and also to ask prayer for the work. He wrote the letter which was to be mimeographed, and showed it to Mrs. Fuller. She approved

89

of the idea, but she suggested that they fill up the page with some good things from her scrap book. So the first letter went out and was warmly received. Word came back from many, assuring them of continued prayer and support.

From then on to the present time, these talks have gone out every two or three weeks, as "Heart-to-Heart Talks," and Mrs. Fuller has greatly enjoyed gathering the material for them. She has thought the name inappropriate and has wanted to change it, but to Mr. Fuller "Heart-to-Heart Talks" is just right. Now many thousands of these letters, carrying messages of comfort and cheer, go out not only all over the United States but to many foreign countries and are eagerly read. One of these Heart-to-Heart Talks is given at the close of this book in order that the readers may see what is sent out, in case they are not among the thousands who receive them regularly.

It now became apparent that God was preparing his faithful servants who were trusting Him through one bitter experience after another for the days ahead when they would be called upon to trust Him to carry on a nation-wide broadcast costing many thousands of dollars each week. They were learning to stand in faith for the smaller things in order that their faith might not fail in the days to come when greater faith would be needed for large funds to carry the Old Fashioned Revival Hour.

After moving to San Marino, Mr. Fuller opened an office in Los Angeles. It was a small room in the Bible

Institute building. Miss Edith McNutt, who had been his secretary when he was pastor of the church in Placentia, came to take charge of that office. She is still with him as his office manager today. He does not forget that when he resigned from Calvary Church, Miss McNutt stood by in those difficult days at a pitifully low salary, assisting in carrying on the radio ministry to which they both felt God had definitely called him. From time to time, as the work has progressed, God has provided other capable, Christian young women to assist in carrying on the work at the offices. Many times the Fullers thank God for these faithful assistants.

Having the vision and working toward a larger radio ministry, Charles Fuller tried an afternoon program on Sunday. He wrote out a twenty minute message, practiced it so that it would go just right and used harp and cello to provide exquisite music. But this rather stereotyped program, lacking as it was in spontaneity, was not the sort of service into which Mr. Fuller could put his heart. So he dropped it. Soon after this he started a Bible class over the radio on Saturday nights, teaching the Sunday school lesson and later giving a series of studies on the typical teaching of the tabernacle worship in the wilderness. He was really feeling around to see just what the Lord had in mind for him for an effective radio ministry. He was not then quite clear as to the program God wanted him to carry forward.

In May, 1933, the Gospel Broadcasting Association was formed. Mr. Fuller wanted to get the growing work on a thoroughly sound business foundation, so that there could be no possible basis for criticism regarding the disposition of funds. He invited a group of about thirty Christian men and women to attend a meeting for organization. From these, twenty-five were appointed as organizers. Application was made for incorporation under the laws of the State of California, with the name, "Gospel Broadcasting Association," in August, 1933. From the group of organizers was chosen a board of nine directors, an executive committee of three members, and an advisory committee which is composed of ministers of southern California well known for their firm stand on the fundamentals of the faith. Mr. Fuller was made Director of the Association and also Chairman of the Advisory Committee.

All funds received are deposited to the credit of the Gospel Broadcasting Association and are checked out over the signatures of two of the executive officers. Contrary to the impression given by the unfriendly or suspicious, Mr. Fuller receives only a modest salary for his services. The receipts and expenditures of the money which is used to carry on the work are accounted for by the most careful methods of modern bookkeeping, and the accounts are audited every ninety days by one of the best known firms of public accountants in America. The auditor who has thus been examining the accounts of the work congratulated Mr. Fuller recently on their scrupulous accuracy.

About the time the Gospel Broadcasting Association

was organized, Mr. Fuller was able to arrange for a half hour weekly broadcast over KFI, in Los Angeles. Soon Station KNX, in Hollywood, was added. Both of these were fifty thousand watt stations. He also continued to carry three different programs over KGER, in Long Beach. For some time he continued with the half hour program over KNX and then, in 1935, decided to try an hour's broadcast over this powerful station which covered the eleven western states, western Canada, and Alaska, even reaching east of the Rockies in some places. He engaged the auditorium of the Hollywood Women's Club for these trial broadcasts, at a cost of $350 a week, which was then considered a tremendous sum. Some of his friends tried to dissuade him, saying that an independent religious program could not be expected to carry such a hookup, with no church or sponsors on which to depend. They said, "Charlie, you haven't any money to carry this, and it will swamp you! You will put yourself deeply into debt." Another remarked, "Fuller won't last six weeks on KNX." But, firmly believing that he was working according to God's plan, he went ahead, saying, "We will undertake it for a month, and see what God will do."

Mrs. Fuller had not been attending the broadcasts which were released from the different studios in the vicinity of Los Angeles. Danny was small then and not very strong. But in this larger venture for which they were both praying much she decided to take a hand. On that first evening she went with Mr. Fuller to the Club in

93

Hollywood. When they arrived, they found a group of about fifty persons who seemed lost in the great auditorium. They called for volunteer singers from the audience and finally had a group of about twelve gathered before the microphone on the platform when they went on the air.

Mrs. Fuller says, of that broadcast, "We were all pretty nervous. None of us were singers, but we did our best and sang lustily, 'with grace in our hearts, to the Lord.' I had slipped over to the control man in the wings, just before we went on the air, and asked him to build up the singing as much as possible. We had determined that this program was to be informal and spontaneous, and it certainly was! Mr. Fuller preached that night with great freedom and conviction. After the broadcast we hurried home to hear how it sounded to Mrs. Barnhill who had remained to listen. We were happy to hear her say that it sounded as though a large group were singing and that she considered the sermon good!"

That was the humble beginning of the Old Fashioned Revival Hour, born in Hollywood, the very place where Mr. Fuller himself had been born again thirteen years before. During the following week, letters approving the program began to pour in from up and down the whole Pacific Coast. With the letters came enough financial assistance to encourage Mr. Fuller to carry on the hour's program until the first of January; and then on and on until the station management was changed, in 1936. The first of January, 1937, he was obliged to switch to the

Mutual Broadcasting System, carrying thirteen stations and extending as far east as Gary, Indiana.

The preaching of the gospel as it was carried out over the air west of Gary, during those months, was greatly blessed of God in reaching the hearts of the people. Letters came in reporting many souls saved and believers comforted and built up in the faith. Charles Fuller rejoiced as he saw God working in such a wonderful way.

But one day in August, 1937, a blow fell. Mr. Alber, the radio agent, came into Mr. Fuller's office saying that an eastern firm was making arrangements with the Mutual network for a coast-to-coast hookup which would include stations that had been releasing the Old Fashioned Revival Hour. He said that, of course, the religious program would have to step aside for such a large hookup. Mr. Fuller looked thoughtfully out of the window. He could not believe that this radio ministry was finished. He felt that God was using it in preparation for a greater ministry. Suddenly he rose to his feet and looking intently at Mr. Alber he said, "Rudy, you tell the Mutual Broadcasting System that the Old Fashioned Revival Hour *will take that network coast-to-coast.*"

The agent looked at him in astonishment and said, "Can you make it, Charlie?"

"No," he replied. "I cannot, but GOD CAN!"

And He did. It was a tremendous step of faith. Mr. Fuller had just five Sundays in which to acquaint his radio audience with the emergency and to enlist their prayers and support. It meant a jump from *13* to *65* stations, and an increase in cost from *$1441* to *$4500* a week. It seemed humanly impossible of accomplishment, for not only must the $1441 each week be carried along to pay for the broadcast being given, but enough extra must come in to take care of the $4500 which would have to be paid for the national hookup the first Sunday in October.

When that night came, the broadcast had been paid for on the previous Friday and *$4.29* was left over in the bank! God had answered prayer. THE OLD FASH-IONED REVIVAL HOUR WAS CARRYING THE GOSPEL OVER THE ETHER WAVES FROM COAST-TO-COAST!

Later, the number of stations was increased to eighty. Then, in October, 1938, the number was raised to one hundred and seventeen. At the present time, more than one hundred and fifty stations release the Old Fashioned Revival Hour each Sunday night, carrying the sweet old story of the gospel to every state in the Union, into the wilderness fastnesses of Canada, to Alaska, Panama, and by short wave to Honolulu and the southern tip of South America. It has been heard by short wave also in Europe and Australia.

The cost of this broadcast and the office expenses amounts to many thousands of dollars each week, a tremendous sum to come in by mail weekly from those who feel impressed to give as unto the Lord. There is no denomination backing this work; there are no sponsors; there are no pledges, and it seems not to be His plan that there should be any surplus. God never has failed to send in the necessary funds, as thousands have prayed all over the land.

Of course, the testings have been many and severe. Some weeks, Mr. Fuller has come up to Thursday and, on one or two occasions even to Friday morning, with almost nothing in the treasury for the coming Sunday broadcast. The check must go in on Friday, in advance of the Sunday program. But in answer to prayer, time after time, God has undertaken and the money has come in miraculously.

On one occasion, when the cost of the broadcast was $500 a week, they came to Friday lacking $150. At this time, the Fullers' beach cottage had been vacant for some time and it seemed that they would have to lose the property unless it could be rented. Mr. Fuller was almost discouraged. As he left the house for the office, Mrs. Fuller went to the home of a dear friend and asked her to come and pray with them. She came gladly, and they had a season of earnest prayer. As they sat at the dinner table the telephone rang. It proved to be a real estate agent, who told her that he had someone who wanted to lease their beach house for a year. Returning to the table with a thankful heart, she was hardly seated when the telephone rang again. A voice which was strange to her said, "Does Mr. Fuller need some financial help for the broadcast next Sunday?"

When Mr. Fuller went out to see the man it proved to be a very successful young dentist who had attended the broadcast of the Pilgrim Hour in Long Beach. He was in a backslidden condition at that time and was brought back into fellowship with God as he listened to the message of Mr. Fuller.

After greeting Mr. Fuller and welcoming him into his home, he said, "How much do you need for next Sunday's broadcast?"

Mr. Fuller replied, with some embarrassment because of the size of the sum, "Well, I am short $150."

This young man turned to his wife with a smile, and said, "Isn't that amazing?"

He took from his pocket a check made out for $150 and handed it to Mr. Fuller. He said that during the night his wife had awakened him saying she felt impressed that they should send Mr. Fuller some money to help carry on the radio ministry. God had directed them as to the amount for which they should make out the check. Needless to say, there was praise and thanksgiving to God for answered prayer that night in the Fuller home.

A large percentage of the cost of this tremendous nation-wide broadcast is supplied by very small gifts. Some contributions of five or ten dollars are received but most are dollar bills sent in by poor people who love the program. These are the gifts which carry the work on from week to week.

Many thousands of letters pour into the office. A great many of these contain words of appreciation and small offerings. But not nearly all. Many are from those whose hearts are torn with sorrow and who need to know the way of comfort and peace; many from those who have wandered far into forbidden paths of sin and who do not know the way out; many from those who need advice in personal matters. All are read and answered. This requires the assistance of several secretaries. The letters are sorted and piled according to the contents. They are personally and prayerfully answered, and often tracts are enclosed which bear on the need.

Everything possible is done to follow up the needy cases and to bring them to the Saviour. A desperate case was noted in a letter recently, when a man wrote that unless he could find relief for the burden of his heart by the next Sunday he would surely commit suicide. Much prayer went up for this man and a letter was written to him and helpful literature sent. On the Sunday evening broadcast, Mr. Fuller asked the listening audience to pray while he made clear to the man God's wonderful provision for his needs. Such follow-up work as this, alone, is worth the entire weekly cost of the broadcast. It is estimated that for every dollar invested twelve hundred listeners are reached with the gospel, and many are converted. It is, surely, the least expensive form of evangelism that it is possible to carry forward today, and deserves the enthusiastic support and earnest prayers of every Christian person in America.

9

A GLIMPSE INTO THE STUDIO ON SUNDAY EVENING

WOULD OUR readers like to attend one of these Sunday evening broadcasts of the Old Fashioned Revival Hour from a large studio of KHJ, in Los Angeles? Perhaps there is no better way to do so than to see it through the eyes of one of Charles Fuller's closest friends, Dr. Charles G. Trumbull, Editor of the *Sunday School Times*, of Philadelphia. No one in America has followed the work of the Old Fashioned Revival Hour with a more solicitous interest than both Dr. and Mrs. Trumbull. Let us, then, go with them as they visit the broadcast.

"On a Sunday evening in August, my wife and I were driving along Seventh Street in Los Angeles, looking for the Don Lee Building. We found it, parked our car, and went in. The salesrooms and business offices were closed, of course, but one elevator was running, and we told the operator we wanted the studio floor. Then we walked along the spacious hallways hunting for our goal, a KHJ studio. From other studios we heard some loud and jazzy singing, so we kept on. Finally we came to a door opening into a big room, and just inside the door we saw a big man. The sense of strangeness dropped away, for the big man had brought our hunt to an end. It was genial, big-bodied, big-hearted, big-souled Charlie Fuller. Into the studio we hurried, and then we saw Mrs. Fuller —"Grace" to Mrs. Trumbull and myself, and from both of them we had the heartiest kind of welcome. I was to see and hear for myself, that evening, something I had long known about but had not yet visited—a broadcasting service of the Old Fashioned Revival Hour.

"The studio was a large, very plain room, perhaps fifty by sixty feet. A block of seats across one side, facing the entrance, took care of about thirty people. Another block of seats at right angles with the first held about the same number; these were the choir, I learned later. There was a grand piano in a far corner, with a vibra-harp in the front-center of the room. While we waited for the service to begin, and while talking with Mr. and Mrs. Fuller and other friends, four young men were standing, their heads close together, singing quietly but with perfectly trained voices some of the old gospel hymns. This was the quartet, whom I had been thrilled to hear over the air and whom I was now to hear face to face. Each one of the quartet is a consecrated Christian, and one or more of them have had tempting offers from motion picture companies, which have been declined on the ground that the Christian life, and evangelistic singing, and the motion picture profession, do not mix.

"Half a dozen microphones were distributed in different parts of the studio, Mr. Fuller's 'mike' and his reading stand being not far from the door where we had first seen him. Another microphone, a dozen feet away, was Mrs. Fuller's 'pulpit.' The rest of the 'mikes' took care of the choir, quartet, piano, and vibra-harp. Still other visitors who came in from time to time were accommodated with chairs, and there must have been a hundred people present when the service was under way. But, while one hundred of us were listening or sharing in that Sunday evening service, those who were listening with us, outside the studio, numbered probably 5,000,000 souls, from California to Maine, from Florida to Alaska, as the six studio microphones carried the prayers, the hymns, the announcements, and the gospel sermon to eighty-five stations of the Mutual Broadcasting System and its affiliated stations throughout North America." (Now, in March, 1940, the listening audience is estimated to be several million more people each week; the stations number 152, and the coverage includes South America, the Islands of the Sea, and even many parts of Asia, besides the remotest sections of North America.)

Conversation quieted, and one could feel the atmosphere of intent, even intense waiting and anticipation, as the big electric clock in plain sight of all showed 7:28, then 7:29. But several minutes before the 'zero hour' had come, Mr. Fuller had led us all in earnest prayer for God's blessing upon the service. Then as the hands of the clock came to 7:30 and the red electric bulb gleamed out, the announcer quietly told the listening millions that the Old Fashioned Revival Hour had begun, and the choir and quartet sang the Theme Song, 'Jesus Saves.'

"As Charles Fuller spoke his opening words to his vast unseen congregation a quiet little smile of welcome was on his face and in his voice, and one felt as though he were just speaking to a little circle of intimate personal friends, instead of to an eager, continent-wide assemblage.

"He was very noticeably the commander-in-chief of his forces during the next sixty minutes. Every two or three minutes he took a look at that clock, for he knew just how much time each hymn, announcement, solo, letter-reading, and every detail should fill. His bearing was alert, electric in its responsibility and leadership. As he came near the end of what he was saying, from time to time, he raised a finger in the direction of the choir or the quartet, or the vibra-harp, as a signal that they were to do their part the instant he stopped speaking. Watching the clock, he knew whether two, or three, or four verses of a hymn should be sung, and this was signaled by the lifting of one or two or more fingers. When he knew that at the end of any verse that selection should stop, he gave the extremely expressive signal of passing his forefinger swiftly across his throat—the signal could be understood even by one who had never been in the studio before!

"The choir singing and the quartet music are a faultless part of this ministry. Leland Green, an accomplished young musician and choir leader who worked with Mr.

Fuller in the Placentia church, is in charge of the Revival Hour music, and is a soloist also with the beautiful vibraharp.

"No part of the program is more eagerly awaited than Mrs. Fuller's personal message and reading from letters received. The whole program is so beautifully human, by the way; nothing stiff, or artificial, or theatrical in it, but just plain home folks talking to one another and talking to you. When Mrs. Fuller's part in the program comes, Mr. Fuller announces it, then says, 'All right, dear,' or 'Go ahead, honey,' just as though he and she were in a little group of half a dozen people instead of millions. But the millions are drawn nearer to the hearts of these dear children of God by these spontaneous, unrehearsed touches."

Here are parts of letters Mrs. Fuller read that Sunday evening in August.

From an Oregon listener came this:

Dear Mr. Fuller: We are so thankful that God has given us a little chance to help with your program, and that we can have a little part in it. My, how we do enjoy the short hour you are on the air! We just pull up our chairs by the radio and feast, but the little hour passes all too quickly, and then we have to wait another whole week. Our little five-year-old girl likes it, too, and all through the week she sings one of your songs—"We Will Understand It Better By and By," —and how true that is! It seems our blessings are so many, even though our income is so very small. We only have two acres of ground and are doing our best to make an honest living on it, though this year we cannot sell our black-berries at all, which should be the largest part of our living; but we had one more milk goat than we needed, and we were able to sell her, so can send you something. Oh, if there were only more goats to sell and more Christians to pray, what a different world this would be! God bless you all and make more like you.

From a man in an Alabama prison came a letter that brought a sober look to faces and an ache to hearts as they listened. It is a letter of combined joy and sorrow.

Dear Friend: Just a few lines to let you hear from me, a friend. As I was reading your Heart-to-Heart Talk which you sent to a friend of mine here, he asked me to write you a few lines as I and him are inmates here in this jail, and as my-self, being a Christian, I am much interested. I have often heard you over the radio before I came here, and I enjoyed listening. It was while reading your Heart-to-Heart Talk that gave me the inspiration to write this letter, but I am not a born letter-writer, and besides, I am under a death sen-tence, and I have been in this jail nearly two years, and since the Supreme Court has affirmed my sentence, they have set my date to die August 19. I mention this only as an intro-duction before starting to reveal what is on my mind. You do not know me, but when I look at your character that pours out between the lines of the paper, I begin to think of you as my friend, because you made me feel uplifted and nearer God . . . Yours in His love, Jimmie Brown.

Dr. Trumbull continues: "Finally comes the heart of the Old Fashioned Revival Hour, Charles Fuller's evan-gelistic sermon. His subject was 'Repentance.' His Scripture: Mark 1:15: 'Repent ye, and believe the gospel.' Luke 13:3: 'Except ye repent, ye shall all likewise perish.' Before beginning the message Mr. Fuller said: 'Between now and our next broadcast will you—all of you—read the thirteenth chapter of Matthew carefully and prayerfully? The thirteenth chapter of Matthew is one of the great mountain-peak chapters of the Bible. Beginning with our next broadcast I am planning a series on chapters 13 and 24 of Matthew, dealing with present-day events in the light of prophecy. Pray for a rich harvest of souls!'

"Then came a rich message, an inescapable one, a convicting one, on Repentance. There were three divisions: The Need of Repentance; Meaning of Repentance; Results of Repentance.

"Plenty of Bible passages threw shafts of light on this theme and each of its divisions, and it was hard to understand how any unsaved soul, among the millions of listeners, could resist God's pleading invitation to accept salvation.

"That God was giving the message through Charles Fuller, no one who watched and listened could doubt. His love of God, love of the Word, love of the Saviour, and love of souls burned in his heart, his voice, his face. He was not watching the clock now—clock and friends and strangers in the studio were forgotten, as God carried him through his message and held him faithful to it. He spoke from carefully prepared notes and outline, of course, and he knew, from experience, how long it would take to give the message, so it was safe for him to forget the clock. Toward the end of the sermon he glanced at the timepiece, and a few minutes later he brought his message to a close.

"And then, after prayer and hymn, the memorable service was over. When the light in the gleaming red electric bulb faded out, the first thing Mr. Fuller did was to lead all in the studio in prayer that God would bless the service just held and use it to the saving of souls."

But we can almost hear some people ask for a little more about those who participate each week in the broadcasts,—Mr. Green, the male quartet and the capable pianist. I know you would be glad to meet them, in person. Since this is impossible for most of you, we are going to give you a brief word picture of them and show you their composite photographs.

Leland Green, the competent choir leader, was converted in one of Mr. Fuller's meetings in Flagstaff, Arizona. He is a graduate of the Bible Institute of Los Angeles and has a Master's degree in music from the University of Southern California. For several years he was connected with the Fullers in their work at Calvary Church in Placentia. The fine choir which sings on the Old Fashioned Revival Hour is a credit to his splendid gift for training and directing gospel singers. And the singing grows better and better. His strong Christian experience is a force for deepening the spiritual life of all who are in the choir.

Rudolph Atwood, at the piano, with his fingers running back and forth across the keyboard so capably, with such a splendid touch, is completing courses at the Bible Institute of Los Angeles. He is no mean speaker, either, and is known throughout southern California as a zealous, energetic witness for Christ. He is tall and slender, full of life and enthusiasm.

Members of the male quartet, a most helpful part of the musical program every Sunday night on the Old Fashioned Revival Hour, have for some time been: Bill MacDougall, first tenor; John Knox, second tenor; Al Harlan, baritone, and Arthur Joissle, bass. But since the first rough draft of this book was written, John Knox, the deeply spiritual second tenor who sang many of the solo parts in the quartet, whose voice was loved and listened to by millions of greatly stirred people from week to week, has been called Home. After a year of failing health, hardly noticeable to any save his close friends, John became very ill. An operation failed to save his life, for it seemed that God wanted to use his beautiful and heart-moving voice in His own heavenly choir. In February (1940), he slipped quietly away. The Sunday evening following the funeral service, a transcription of his rendition of "The Stranger of Galilee" was given over the air. Hundreds wrote in to tell what a blessing the song had been to them, that night, as they listened to those sublime words and thought of that young life that had meant so much to them, as he had sung again and again in the anointing of the Spirit, straight into their hearts.

One and another is being substituted in his place, but

it is very difficult for anyone to fill the place which he has left vacant. His very life was a benediction. His prayers in the studio were always such a blessing. He was like another son to the Fullers, and they miss him greatly.

This quartet has been composed of genial, talented, and spiritual young fellows. Every morning their voices are heard singing, as Rudolph Atwood plays for them in a program which was carried on for many years by Rev. Will Hogg and his wife, over another station. In two services on Sunday and at the midweek prayer service they are found actively participating in the regular meetings held at the Little Country Church in Hollywood. There, one evening, we heard them give most earnest personal testimonies as to their faith in the Lord Jesus Christ as their Saviour. They spoke especially of His keeping power day by day, of their great joy in service for Him and their earnest desire to win others to Christ. Mr. Atwood, especially, told of the wonderful time of fellowship they had had that morning in prayer as they had cried to God for an anointing upon them to win souls.

It means increased spiritual power and blessing that all who participate in the Old Fashioned Revival Hour are earnest Christians, praying as they sing, praying as Mr. Fuller speaks, and as Mrs. Fuller reads the heart-warming letters and earnest pleas for spiritual help. God bless them, every one!

10

GREAT PUBLIC GATHERINGS

Ever since Mr. Fuller commenced the Old Fashioned Revival Hour broadcasts he has been besieged with letters inviting him to speak in churches, in halls, and in great mass meetings, all over the country. Most of these he has had to refuse, because of the limit of time and of strength. Occasionally, however, he has accepted calls. In the earlier days of the broadcast he carried on evangelistic campaigns almost continuously, speaking a great deal. But the demands of his work were so great that his strength and time would not permit, and he was forced to drop all protracted meetings.

It is not Mr. Fuller's ability as an orator that enables him to draw the largest audiences on the continent today —audiences equal to the great congregations which used to listen to "Billy" Sunday. It is not because of his amazing personality or because of the remarkable, new things which he says. He is not a dramatic speaker; he is not an orator; he is not a professional evangelist. The secret is that he is Spirit-filled. It is because he presents the simple gospel story in a form which humble, needy hearts can grasp. He is one of the best known and best loved men in America today, largely because he has been the means of bringing many thousands to Christ, of stirring the sluggish, nearly spiritually dead souls of many thousands more, and of bringing cheer and blessing to hosts of others. When he is in town every one of his listeners in that area wants to be sure to see him and hear him "in person" and they bring along their friends and relatives, too. It is not an idolatrous adulation. They are his friends; they are the ones whom he has blessed with his messages; they are the ones who love him because he tells them of Christ. Christ, after all, is the drawing power, and the message of the gospel, plainly and interestingly told, is the reason for their coming.

In December, 1937, the Christian Business Men's Committee of Chicago invited him to hold a meeting in the Chicago Civic Opera House. A crowd of 6,000 thronged the place. The blessing of God was manifestly felt and many decisions resulted.

A group of Fundamental churches in Des Moines, Iowa, called him to speak in a great meeting at the Civic Auditorium, and 5,800 attended. The Christian Business Men's Committee of Seattle called him to their Civic Auditorium. Portland, and other places as well were asking for meetings, so an itinerary was worked out. It was summer time, in 1938. Time for a vacation! But Charles Fuller never takes much of a vacation. A day or two here and there is all he feels he can spare from the Lord's work. He has never missed a broadcast, winter or summer, for a vacation. For thirteen years, every Sunday night has found him before the microphone giving out the gospel message, with the exception of two Sunday nights when he was ill.

So, when calls came for these summer gatherings, the Fullers decided that Mr. Fuller should fill the engagements but should take Mrs. Fuller and Dan along, doing a little sightseeing together between the meetings. The Seattle gathering was most fruitful. Services were conducted in many smaller cities and towns, through Oregon, Washington and British Columbia. Great mass meetings were held in Vancouver and in Victoria, well attended in spite of unprecedented heat. Many souls were won for Christ. From the great Civic Auditorium of Portland, Oregon, the Sunday evening Old Fashioned Revival Hour was broadcast with a record attendance. Only eternity will show the number born into the Kingdom during that trip.

One of the high spots during 1938 was the meeting in Detroit. There the churches united in a great Good Friday service. The Olympia Stadium was engaged and two mass meetings were held. It was estimated that considerably over 12,000 packed the Stadium both times. Detroit is still talking about it. When that vast audience, on Good Friday afternoon, arose and sang, accompanied by the great pipe organ, "When I Survey the Wondrous Cross," it was most heart-moving and brought tears to many eyes. The invitation was given and people came down even from the second balcony, seeking God. There was a repetition of the same thing that night.

On Easter Sunday morning about 40,000 people gathered in Soldier's Field in Chicago. In the huge coliseum, two thousand trained voices led by a large pipe organ were raised in praise to God. As the invitation was given, in the gray light of that Easter dawn, Mr. Fuller realized that he would be unable to see the hands raised in response to the invitation, so he asked all who wished to accept Christ as Saviour to wave their programs. It was thrilling to see, all over that vast audience, the flutter of white paper programs! There were spaces to be filled in by the new converts, on the programs. Several hundred names were received by the committee and were followed up.

We will let Mrs. Fuller tell you of one amusing incident of that Easter service: "Of course, I was praying for Mr. Fuller as he spoke, as many others were doing. In fact, there had been some all-night prayer meetings there in Chicago. The committee was very much pleased with the definiteness of the message, and I, too, thought it was very good. It was the Word of God given simply, and the Holy Spirit was using it that morning. As I came out through the long tunnel, after the service, I heard a woman say to her companion, 'Well, I don't think he was much of a speaker. He used the same word *twice* in one sentence, and his vocabulary was not brilliant—in fact, it was rather limited.'

"I smiled to myself as I looked at her. She was nice

looking, and I should like to have remarked, 'No, if you came to hear a brilliant orator, that man from California certainly disappointed you! But if you were a sinner needing a Saviour, you might have found the way to Him this Easter morning.' I thought of First Corinthians, chapter two, where Paul says, 'And I, brethren, when I came to you, came not with excellency of speech or of wisdom, declaring unto you the testimony of God. For I determined not to know anything among you, save Jesus Christ, and Him crucified. And I was with you in weakness, and in fear, and in much trembling. And my speech and my preaching was not with enticing words of man's wisdom, but in demonstration of the Spirit and of power.'

"Some people like to hear man lauded and praised, and it wasn't pleasing to some of them to have Mr. Fuller tell them they were *dead* in trespasses and sins—dead, if they were outside of Christ. But it was the power of God which brought conviction to those hearts, that Easter morning."

During the brief four months from the time of the Chicago meeting with the Christian Business Men's Committee until the return visit on Easter morning, over 4,000 decisions for Christ were recorded in those mass meetings. And from reports which we have since received we know that a host of these were truly converted, for their lives bear evidence.

In September, 1938, Mr. Fuller addressed a great meeting at the Hippodrome, in Waterloo, Iowa. Morning and evening, on that humid and stormy day, 10,200 people crowded into the building, and many souls were saved. The Hippodrome has a corrugated iron roof. It had been raining intermittently all day and, as the time for the evening service drew near, it was coming down in torrents, making a great noise on the metal roof. The Old Fashioned Revival Hour was to be released from that building and, a few minutes before time to go on the air, Mr. Fuller realized that unless the rain ceased the broadcast going from coast to coast would be ruined. It looked as though the rain might continue all night. He walked over to the technician's desk and listened through the ear phones. There was just a loud roar. There was nothing Mr. Fuller could do except to pray. As he walked to the front of the platform, Satan said to him, "Suppose, when you pray, the rain does not stop! They will laugh you out of town!"

He lifted his hand, asking the great audience to pray with him as he said, "Father, in Jesus' name will you please stop the rain that this broadcast may go out clearly for Thy glory."

And, just as though a faucet were being turned off, the rain stopped! And none fell until ten minutes after the broadcast was over. Then it fell in such torrents that the crowds could not leave for a time. People were greatly impressed and many were brought to the Lord because of what they had seen of God's power.

In October, 1938, the Christian Business Men's Committee of San Francisco held a mass meeting in the Civic Auditorium of that city with Charles Fuller as speaker.

The place was filled to capacity. It was another moving service, with many conversions.

After years of incessant labors in the Lord's vineyard both day and night, in season and out of season, Mr. Fuller's health began to show the effects of the strain. His strength seemed almost gone, especially after the broadcast or some great meeting; his heart was not as strong as it used to be, and his resistance was low. The doctor became alarmed over the depletion of his strength and ordered a complete rest and change. Mr. Fuller could not leave his radio ministry. It was too near to his heart, too much a part of his very life, too important to millions of listeners each week. He simply could not give that up. For thirteen years he had missed only two Sundays of broadcasting. A wonderful record! But he finally consented to cancel his winter engagements outside and endeavor to take more rest during the week. Leaving his faithful comrade in all of his labors to stand by in prayer for the income so much needed each week, he slipped away into the desert to a little cabin retreat where he could be alone with God and regain his vigor. It was almost more than he could do—to leave the work for even two or three days each week, but it had to be done, if he were not to go under completely. So, for months, the weekly program found him leaving on Monday for a brief rest, then back again Thursday or Friday to prepare once more for the broadcast on Sunday night.

The rest was doing him good—not bringing about a

complete recovery as had been hoped, but at least building up greater resistance.

In the late fall, the New England Fellowship began to send urgent invitations for the Fullers to visit New England, to put on a series of mass meetings in strategic centers. Mr. Fuller's physicians would not permit so extensive a program as this; but they finally consented to the trip East, and to his taking engagements in New York and Philadelphia as well as one day in Boston. In March, 1939, it was decided that the Evangelistic Association of New England should join with the New England Fellowship in sponsoring two great meetings in Mechanics Building, Boston, on May 7.

It had been many years since Mr. and Mrs. Fuller had been East to see the early home of their parents. Dan, too, was eager to view all the sights and to take pictures with his new camera. So all three made the trip, starting right after their Sunday broadcast on April 30. Their first stop was in Philadelphia, with their close friends, Dr. and Mrs. Charles G. Trumbull. Dan was taken seriously ill with an ear infection which held Mrs. Fuller there for several days. Mr. Fuller flew to Boston with the "control man" who had guided him safely through the radio channels ever since the Old Fashioned Revival Hour first went over the Mutual Broadcasting System.

May we pause a moment to give you a glimpse of this God-given addition to the group which carries forward this great broadcast. In the early days of the Mutual

Broadcasting System and of the Old Fashioned Revival Hour, when Mr. Fuller was young in this "game" of broadcasting, an energetic, fine appearing young man came to him, one day, to get acquainted. He was just commencing what has turned out to be one of the finest careers on the coast as a radio manager for various programs. He seemed to know his business, he had a clean, strong face, and Mr. Fuller liked him. He was not a Christian at the time, but was interested in what Mr. Fuller was attempting to do. He said, "Mr. Fuller, I should like to handle your radio programs, to be your 'contact man' with the radio world. I know the business and you don't. You ought to have a radio man and I'd be glad to take over the job."

It was a deal. Mr. R. H. Alber made the necessary arrangements with the Mutual Broadcasting System for the first thirteen station broadcast of the Old Fashioned Revival Hour. This was the first of January, 1937, and they have been together ever since. The Mutual Broadcasting System has grown rapidly; Mr. Fuller's program has grown also, and Mr. Alber has become a great figure in America as an expert radio contact man. God gave him to the Old Fashioned Revival Hour. Through the simple, heart stirring messages to which he listened his own heart has been touched and he has become a sincere Christian. He and Mr. Fuller are brothers together in giving out the gospel to millions, one through the message, the other through the myriad, amazingly complicated details of managing the business end of a great radio hookup.

There are constant changes to be made, as Mr. Alber watches the various graphs which are kept, indicating the listening audience in different localities. Always he is working to reach the greatest number of listeners for the lowest cost. All of this work is carried on in a strictly business-like way. Radio officials have said, "We cannot get such accurate information as to percentages, averages, and so forth from any other program in the country. Your charts and graphs show everything in black and white, and that gives information which leads to the best results."

Every one of the four hundred or more stations must be contacted and all arrangements made for the program; the lines must be cleared; details as to buying the time worked out; and in the broadcast itself every particular in connection with the studio, microphones, connections and controls must be perfected. Mr. Alber goes everywhere with Mr. Fuller when a Sunday night broadcast is to be given from some other city than Los Angeles. So he came to Boston—a fine, quiet, efficient business man who arranged all the details for the coming program.

Mechanics Building in Boston was almost entirely filled by the time Mr. Fuller arrived on the aforesaid evening of May 7. Mr. Allen C. Emery, president of the Evangelistic Association presided over the meeting. Mr. William Turkington, a song leader and evangelist under the same organization, stood before the great audience and the mixed choir on the platform to lead the singing. Mr. Philip Geary's nimble fingers played rippling melodies up and down the keyboard. Other musicians of the New England Fellowship were on the platform. Everything was set and everyone was there except Mrs. Fuller. It looked as though the audience would be disappointed by not seeing her. Suddenly, as Mr. Fuller was making a few preliminary remarks, he stopped short and said, with a glad ring in his voice, "There she is. Come right up, honey, to the platform."

And, sure enough, Mrs. Fuller was coming in, away at the back of the auditorium, too far for many on the platform to see her. Soon she was at her husband's side, participating in the service.

It was a great meeting. Mr. Fuller gave an account of the Old Fashioned Revival Hour and of God's wonderful answers to prayer, for before him were his friends, those who had listened to him through the years and wanted to hear all about it. Then an offering was taken for the broadcast, after which Mr. Fuller gave a heart searching message on salvation. Many came forward to accept the Lord as their Saviour, personal workers dealt with them, and the service was dismissed.

In the later evening, after church services in Boston, another large crowd gathered for the regular broadcast of the Old Fashioned Revival Hour, this time from Mechanics Building in Boston. The hastily drilled chorus, under Mr. Turkington's direction, sang out, "Jesus Saves," and the broadcast was on. Mr. Fuller directed it much as he does in the studio in Los Angeles. The musicians were different but the good old gospel songs were the same.

THE LADY WITH THE CHARMING VOICE—
MRS. CHARLES E. FULLER

A RECENT PICTURE OF MRS. LEONORA BARNHILL

Leaders of the sponsoring organizations spoke brief words of greeting, Mrs. Fuller read some stirring letters, and Mr. Fuller preached. After the broadcast, others came forward on Mr. Fuller's invitation, to accept Christ and to pledge themselves anew to Him.

Following the service, a man stepped up to Mr. Fuller and introduced himself. He said, "Mr. Fuller, I was a professional gambler. I was in a joint where I had just made $1500 in gambling and was gathering up my ill gotten gains when suddenly, as the program which we were hearing changed, your broadcast of two weeks ago came over the air. I would have turned it off, when I realized it was a religious program, but I had a praying mother and those old songs she used to sing sounded mighty sweet. I told the boys to leave it on awhile, and they did. I listened, and we stopped playing cards pretty soon. I heard your sermon. I knew I was a black sinner; I hated the life I was living. I accepted Christ at the end of your sermon, and pushing the $1500 in winnings across the table, I said, 'Boys, you can take it. I'm through with all this,' and I left. I've started a new life and I'm going to meet my dear mother over there."

He went out of that gambling den a changed man, a new creature in Christ Jesus. When he heard the Fullers were to be in Boston he determined to go there and tell them what Christ had done for him through their message. How it encouraged the hearts of these servants of the Lord, tired after ministering so faithfully and truly to 10,000 or more people in Boston!

On Monday night, Mr. and Mrs. Fuller were guests of honor at the annual dinner of the New England Fellowship in the crypt of St. Paul's Cathedral. During the week, they saw many old landmarks around New England, much to the delight of Dan who had recovered sufficiently to join them.

The following Sunday night's broadcast was to be from New York. Mr. Fuller had been asked by the Christian Business Men's Committee for the World's Fair to open the services which were to be conducted every night during the summer at Calvary Baptist Church, in New York. But when plans were being made it was evident that the auditorium of the church would not begin to seat the vast crowd desiring to attend the service. So Carnegie Hall was engaged and notices of the change were hastily sent out to Christian leaders and newspapers.

Sunday afternoon, May 14, Carnegie Hall was packed to the highest galleries. When asked how many people listened in to the Old Fashioned Revival Hour there was a sea of hands waving enthusiastically. So, again, Mr. Fuller told of God's wonderful provision throughout the years and of blessing received, then gave a gospel message and invitation. In the evening also, the Hall was filled for the great service. There was an overflow meeting via public address system in Calvary Baptist Church, which followed the service conducted by Dr. William Ward Ayer, pastor of that church. Millions listened to the service as it was broadcast from 9:00 to 10:00, E.S.T. It was a great day and a real answer to prayer.

Philadelphia, hearing of the vast crowds in Boston and in New York, changed their arrangements and engaged a larger auditorium. They had a fine meeting there, and in Washington, D. C., as well, with really blessed results. Then the Fullers returned to Los Angeles, glad to be back at the studio, in spite of the intense heat, on the evening of May 28.

Detroit was calling for another service, so it was arranged that there should be a large mass meeting on Belle Isle, the famous resort of Detroit, on the Fourth of July, 1939. The trip included fine meetings at Winona Lake, and in Iowa, where thousands heard the gospel in services long to be remembered.

The summer was, frequently, a time of testing, because of the many new stations added in 1939 and the new friends who had not yet learned to help financially. But God wonderfully saw them through the season with all bills paid. It was a miraculous answer to prayer. In the fall the strain seemed even greater, and the gifts were sometimes not sufficient, up to the last moment, to meet the tremendous expenses.

The strain has been telling on Mr. Fuller. Plans made last year to return to New England for a series of mass meetings in Lewiston, Lynn, Lowell, Providence, Hartford, Portland, and other cities, in connection with the New England Fellowship, had to be cancelled, and Mr. Fuller was obliged again to go into retirement whenever he could be spared for brief seasons of rest and quiet. Physicians are insistent that he shall not attempt anything beside his radio ministry and office schedule. All outside engagements are cancelled. They urge a month or two of complete change away from every care but Mr. Fuller will not listen to the suggestion for a moment.

So the Old Fashioned Revival Hour goes on. Much prayer is needed for this ministry; prayer for those who listen and are touched and need to surrender to God; prayer for the weary and sad and discouraged; prayer for the new born Christians so often without any spiritual help except as they hear the message on Sunday nights; and especially earnest prayer for the Fullers, that grace and strength may be given them for this great work. They need constant, united and prevailing prayer. Let us not fail them as they carry on for God!

11

MRS. FULLER STEPS TO THE "MIKE"

THE READING by Mrs. Fuller of some of the thousands of letters that come, each week, is one of the high spots of the broadcast. The helpfulness of this part of the service is greatly enhanced by her sympathetic comments. She is blessed with one of the most musical voices heard on any program. We will let her take the microphone. As Mr. Fuller would say, "Go ahead, honey."

"Here is an interesting letter from Chicago, and just below the signature it says, 'Born in 1881, no learning.' Well, God bless her. The letter is hard to read, but I get the thought she wishes to express; that she loves the broadcast; she loves to listen, and that through listening she has come to know right from wrong, and the love of God has come into her heart. She says, 'Rev. Fuller: This comes to you and members. I don't know what you all are, whether you are white or not, but I am not doing nothing that is wrong. My spirit leads me as I listen to your air meetings, and your preaching makes plain God's

Word and now I feel like a new born one. I am straight
with the Lord. If I live I thank God, and if I die I thank
God. Thank you; you make plain the Bible. My trust
is in·God that you can stay on the air. Before I did not
know what was wrong; now the Spirit tells me and I am
changed. Pray for me.'

"Well, bless her heart. Yes, we are all white folks on
this program, but the black folks are God's children, too,
if they are washed in the blood of Christ. We are all one
in Him. Friends, I ask you to pray for this colored
woman in Chicago who has not had the opportunities
that we have had but who has come into great riches as
she has come to know Christ.

"Here is a fine letter from a fourteen year old boy in
Little Woody, Sask., Canada. I just love this: 'Dear
Brother Fuller: Every Sunday night I try to get my
chores done early so I can listen to the Old Fashioned Revival Hour. I think it is the most wonderful program on
the air. Most of last week our radio wasn't working, so I
felt bad because I thought I could not hear you Sunday
night. This morning, Mother accidentally fixed it. I
couldn't help thanking the Lord for allowing us to hear
you. I am enclosing a small contribution and would like
to have the Heart-to-Heart Talks. Yours affectionately,'
and then signed his name 'Walter.' I love to think of that
fourteen year old boy in Canada so enjoying our program
that he thanked God when his mother was able to accidentally fix their radio.

"I love this letter. 'Dear Mr. Fuller: This donation is

small but I give it gladly and pray that it may be acceptable to help in your Bible teaching, which by listening one
month has caused me to find Christ as my Saviour. My
husband and I haven't much money. We have two small
children and we live in a little house at the edge of town.
We owe several bills and a month ago we were filled with
despair. Our bills weren't paid, our children needed
medical care, and we had other worries that seemed to pile
up and up. Four weeks ago I discovered your program
and the following Sunday evening I listened to it again
and resolved that I wanted Christ for my friend. I began
to pray, not very well perhaps, but very sincerely, and my
prayers have been answered. From that day I have found
strength to meet my burdens and help to handle the hard
situations. My husband has been more cheerful too, since
we learned to pray and learned that peace comes in seeking the Lord. May God bless you and the work you are
doing.' Signed, 'A Friend.'

"And, now, I am going to ask Geneva and John to sing
a song for all the lonely ones and those who are filled with
despair. For all those who need a friend,—and there are
many in radioland, they will sing, 'No, Never Alone,'
with Rudy at the little organ. . . .

"A good letter from Saskatchewan, Canada: 'Dear Mr.
Fuller: I live in a district where we have had ten years of
drought, so we farmers have had no crops. I am sorry I
have no money to send, but how we do enjoy your program, and pray you may be blessed in carrying it on. I
would like to have a radio log, if you send them to people

who have no money to send. Thanking you, and God bless you in your work.'

"Well, we certainly send them gladly, and we are so thankful that this program can be carried to those who need it so much, whether they can help any with the expense or not. We rejoice to know, tonight, that we are reaching into the hearts and homes of thousands,—yes, hundreds of thousands, where the need is so great, for one reason or another. Oh, may God make this program always a great blessing to every needy heart, and especially to the very poor!

"Here is a good letter from an Indian evangelist in the North. 'Dear Brother Fuller: Just before going to church, last night, where I am conducting a revival meeting, I tuned in on your program. I wish to say I received a great blessing from your sermon. I took my Bible and followed as you read the 140th Psalm. Brother Fuller, that sermon was for me. I sat there and cried all through it. Here is the reason I wept. For one month I have been going through one of the darkest hours of my life. The heavens have seemed like brass but, glory to His name, I heard His voice speaking through you, last night, and it gave me new life to go ahead. I'm not a great preacher but I am trying to fill the place where God has placed me. I've been saved over fifteen years. I am a Chippawa Indian from Ontario, Canada. I have been in the Northwest a year. I shall be preaching, next week, for the Indians in the Yakima Indian Reservation.'

"Mr. Fuller was so delighted to hear that this Indian

Dr. and Mrs. Charles E. Fuller and Dan

brother in Christ had been cheered and inspired to go on preaching the Word, as Mr. Fuller brought it to him there so far away. And I ask you to pray with us for this dear man, that God may encourage him in just the needed way and that he may see real fruit for his labor. You know Satan does buffet and hinder all who are standing true in these days, and we should pray much one for another. You will pray with us for this Indian evangelist, won't you?

"Here is an interesting letter from a young man in Maine who is in the United States Field Artillery, clear across the country. He has listened to the Old Fashioned Revival Hour just two Sunday nights and writes that he has become much interested. He says, 'I feel that right now my greatest need is Christ. My past is black with sin. I have been drinking and, as a whole, I have been a very great sinner. I feel that if this country should be drawn into the war of course I will be one of the first to go, and I also feel that I should go. But I would dislike going to the front without knowing that I was a child of God. Since I've listened to your message I have thought it all over and I would like to become a Christian. I will be thirty-one years old next Saturday. Will you please pray for me. I will be more than pleased to hear from you. You don't think it's too late for me to come to Christ, do you?'

"We've been praying for this young man and a letter has gone to him telling him it is certainly not too late. We are doing what we can to make the way of salvation a little clearer. We hope that he may be able to continue to listen and pray that he will come out into a clear accept- ance of Christ as his Saviour.

"Here is a pathetic letter. It is not signed. 'Dear Rev. Fuller: My humble request is for your prayers. I am an unsaved person. For over ten years I have had a great longing for God, but this longing has never been satisfied. I am still without Christ. I attend church, but I am a hypocrite. I want to be a true Christian. My life is use- less, is desperately unhappy—so lonely and discontented. I do not know what peace is. I am always troubled. My godly mother died when I was a young girl. Grieving for her has brought many premature grey hairs to my head, for I am without comfort or guide in my life. A certain hymn goes like this, 'There is Wonderful Power in the Blood.' That is my only wish, that God bestow that saving power on my soul. Dear people of God, won't you, by the mercies of God, pray for me? God knows my identity though I do not sign this letter.'

"Friends, will you join with me in prayer for this trou- bled soul? Hearts are so hungry, these days, seeking for God. That is one of the thrills of the radio, that it reaches folks just where they are. Oh, yes, people are being saved. We have many letters, but the pity of it is that many do not write us. A Bible teacher told me, this week, that two young people are in a Bible training school, in her classes, and they told her they were converted by lis- tening to the Old Fashioned Revival Hour. She said, 'I meet dozens and dozens of people, as I go about, who tell me they have accepted the Lord through listening over the air to your program.' But I do wish they would all write us and let us help them."

And the lady with the lovely radio voice, on June 12, 1938, said: "Friends, I don't know what we would do without the sacrificial help of the radio friends as we get into the summer months. Your letters tell how you are doing without things, when many of you have so little, because you want the Lord's work carried on and souls won. These letters are a real inspiration and I wish I could read every one over the air. I feel more confident than ever that, with this spirit of sacrifice, we are going to be able to keep our Hour which is so expensive, and also take the other stations necessary to hold it next fall and winter.

"We appreciate the way people, in this crisis time, are sacrificing to help. One dear old lady who is very ill with arthritis and hasn't walked in over two years sent her offering earned from patching, and one lady makes quilts and sent her offering from the sale of a quilt. A lady in Wisconsin was ill. She prayed for the Lord to heal her so that she would not have to spend her money for doctor bills. He did touch her body, so she sent her money to the Old Fashioned Revival Hour. One woman was going to get some ice cream, so she denied herself that and sent fifteen cents. A son-in-law gave his mother 50¢ for Mother's Day and she sent that. Another had a birthday dollar. A lady in South Dakota sent an extra 30¢ saved by buying cotton hose instead of silk; and there was a sweet letter from a girl in Omaha who was lying on a divan listening to the radio. She had a new hat, a beautiful hat which had just been delivered and had not even been taken out of the box. She writes, 'Oh, Mr. and Mrs. Fuller, that hat was a dream,—all but the price. Every time I thought of that I faced reality and my dream came crashing. It was a very expensive hat, but then I told myself that I didn't buy hats very often and so felt justified in buying a good one. But that was just an excuse, and it soon became too weak to lean on. By the time your service had reached the half-way mark I had put the hat back in its box, after a last inspection, so that the messenger boy could pick it up in the morning. That done, I sat down and really enjoyed the rest of your service.' So she had some extra money to send.

"Here is a lovely letter from an old lady in Waterloo, Iowa. She says, 'I had been taking a taxi to church, six blocks away, and I thought I might walk and save a little taxi fare. I am in my eighty-fifth year, and I do not do much walking, but I stand up very well, and am so glad to give this much for the cause of Christ.' Isn't that wonderful!

"Here is one from Memorial Day, money that was to have been used for flowers. 'They will bloom in Heaven now in memory of the departed loved ones.' That's lovely, isn't it? I know this lady and she has quite recently laid away her only little son.

"A woman writes, 'One Monday we went without meat and saved fifty cents. The next Monday I went without coffee and saved ten cents. . . . How I did love the Heart-to-Heart Talk of May 14th. I always give them away, but this one I think I shall have to keep.'

"A man writes from Detroit, 'Today, my wife and I intended to go to a double-header ball game between Detroit and St. Louis, which would cost us $1.10 at the bleechers. We decided to stay home and hear the game over the radio and send that amount to help keep you on the air.'

"Here's a lovely letter from an elderly person in Tacoma, Washington. She loves the program and is so anxious to sacrifice. She had laid aside ten cents to meet a bill. She prayed definitely about it and some provision was made so she didn't have to pay that. Then she went on a call for the Lord and had to ride one way, but the friend brought her back, so she laid her carfare home aside. She goes on to say, 'Today, I went out to get some food for my cat and the butcher gave it to me, so there was another nickel, praise the Lord.' She sent that extra quarter, bless her heart. I just love her letter. I wish I could read you all three pages of it, for every word is good. She certainly knows the Lord.

"Then here is a letter which brings sadness to our hearts, because it tells of the home-going of one of our dear radio friends who has written us so often. Just a few weeks ago she sent me some wash cloths and towels she had crocheted around the edge, though she was blind. She did beautiful work, too. Oh, how we are rejoicing for her that she is at home with the Lord and that she went quickly and didn't have to suffer, but we certainly are going to miss Grandma Wickstrom.

"Here is a pathetic letter from a young girl in Oklahoma: 'I listen to your Old Fashioned Revival Hour and I think it's great. I am a sinner and I want to be saved through the blood of Jesus Christ. Could you send me a Bible with big print, as my eyes are bad and I can't read little print at all. I have no daddy, and my mother has seven of us children. We are very poor and she is not able to get us a Bible. Please remember us in your prayers.' That does touch our hearts and we certainly pray for this family. I shall see that this young girl has a Bible she can read. And I ask listeners to pray, too, for this family.

"You know, a few Sunday nights ago Mr. Fuller introduced me and said that he was getting to be known as Mrs. Fuller's husband. I never know what he's going to say and it puts me in a funny position to know what to say. A man who evidently likes a joke has written, from Mississippi, and he says, 'Dear Husband of Mrs. Fuller: Well, it looks as though Mrs. Fuller is going to make something out of you, after all. Mrs. Fuller read of a lady who listened to your sermon on Presumptuous Sins and stopped smoking cigarettes. I am not sure whether or not that was the sermon, but I do know that during one of your sermons I was trying to pray for my son and my cigarette fogged me so that I had to stop my prayer and at the same time I lost connection with your sermon. Maybe it was just to get even, but I didn't like the idea of a cigarette interfering with my prayers, so I have stopped cigarettes. That was at 9:45 P.M., September 24th. It is not altogether easy to break a habit of more than fifty years, but the Lord undertook and the habit is gone entirely. I am firmly convinced it would be a presumptuous sin for me to smoke again.'

"A copy of a religious paper was sent to us, published in the territory of Hawaii, in which is a very interesting account of the conversion of a young Japanese girl. The first part of the article tells of this young woman's struggle and resistance of the Holy Spirit's wooing and of her refusal to accept Christ. The young lady is reported to have said: 'One Sunday, over the radio, I heard Rev. Fuller's Old Fashioned Revival Hour coming from the States. He spoke of salvation and made it very clear. For a few moments I sat still before the radio thinking how much I would miss and have to give up if I accepted the Lord. Months passed and still my mind was beset by fears and turmoil.' And then she relates that later she came out into a clean cut conversion, and how great was her joy!"

On July 3rd, 1939, the radio voice of Mrs. Fuller was heard to say, "Good evening, friends. I missed being with you all last Sunday night. We were camping in Yosemite Valley and though Mr. Fuller wanted me to come out with him for the broadcast, I just could not leave the boys there alone,—our Dan and his chum. I wanted to hear the program, though, so I started out about two hours before time to see whom I could ask to let me listen in on his car radio. There were many radios in Camp Fifteen, but it took courage to ask such a favor of a stranger. I want to tell you what an amusing experience I finally had. I spoke to two women who sat alone in front of a tent. I said, 'Do you have a radio in your car, and would you mind turning it on for me at 7:30 for a little while? There is a program I am eager to hear at that time.'

"One of them said, 'Is it the Fuller program—the Old Fashioned Revival Hour from Los Angeles? We always listen to that.'

"I said, 'Yes, that is the one I want to hear too.'

"She replied, 'We will gladly tune in for you. I have met both Mr. and Mrs. Fuller.'

"I thought, 'My, how glad I am not to be recognized,' for I was the grimiest sort of camper. Then she said, 'I am Mrs. B. from Pasadena, and this is Mrs. A.'

"My reply was, 'How do you do, Mrs. B. and Mrs. A. Isn't the Valley beautiful, this year, and how lovely the azaleas are,' and I got away without being recognized. When I returned some time later to listen to the program, she said, 'Your voice is very like Mrs. Fuller's as we hear it over the air.' And then, of course, I had to tell them who I was.

"And now for some letters—"

12

THESE HEARD AND BELIEVED

THERE IS no room for doubt that the Old Fashioned Revival Hour is producing definite fruit in great abundance. The following testimonies speak eloquently of the power of God's Word to transform lives even when that Word is projected through the trackless ether waves across a sea or a continent.

A man of ninety-four years finds great joy: We live on a farm five miles from town, me and my husband and my husband's father, and we don't get to attend church services much, especially in the winter. His father is ninety-four years old, and blind. About six months ago he had a very serious sick spell and lost his sight, and was bed-fast for about six months. He didn't know anything about half of the time, but it seemed that he would remember your Hour and would ask us to get the "Old Time Religion" for him. That is what he calls your Hour. I have been saved for about six years and have kept praying God to save him. Well, he got well from that sick spell and he accepted Christ after your program, one night. God took the tobacco habit from him that he had had for eighty years, and he has never tasted tobacco since last July 6th, which was his ninety-fourth birthday. We were all alone and spent the day in prayer and praise to God, and he said it was the happiest birthday he had ever had. He just looks forward to your Hour all through the week. He goes to bed early on Sunday, but just as soon as he hears the singing he gets up and stays up until your Hour is over. Every place I take him he tells people about the "old time religion in California." This is his testimony: that God can and will save and take away all bad habits. Please pray for us that we will have a Christian home that will be a testimony for God.

Dear Mr. Fuller: A little over a month ago I was at wit's end corner, not knowing which way to turn. It took your gospel talk of Sunday, a week ago, to bring me to Christ. Your message seemed just for me.

Not under law, but under grace: I am thankful that God still permits us to hear you. Before we heard you speaking on "Regeneration," Feb. 19, my future Christian life seemed so terribly black. Everywhere I turned it seemed like "Reformation" was pointing its finger at me, saying, "Keep the law; reform; you're lost if you don't obey every commandment." With all these things going on in my mind I was really a stumbling block to my husband. I knew that keeping every law was impossible without Christ Jesus and the new birth. But here I was thinking myself a fine Christian and teaching reform, reform, to my husband. Well, your message from God's Word was such a wonderful blessing to us; it just cleared up the whole thing so beautifully and peacefully that I can't praise Him enough. We truly were very miserable until that wonderful message came. I'm taking this opportunity to thank you. God answered my prayer and sent the message we both needed so much . . . Since the Good Friday service at Olympia Stadium I've settled a misunderstanding over four years old, and how different I feel!

From the Canal Zone: I am a resident of a small country district of Panama. For several months I have been listening to your Sunday evening services and have always enjoyed them and asked my friends to listen. But it was not until Sunday, July 16th, that I came to realize that I was a guilty sinner and that if I did not respond to my Master's call I would be a complete cast-out. Just as the invitation was given out I found myself kneeling beside my radio. Christ accepted me and cleansed me from my sins. I felt so happy in my soul and wanted a full supply of His blessing, so I went immediately to the leaders of a near-by church and asked them to come and rejoice with me. I am glad to report that, from then until now, I have been closely following in His footsteps. I am poor and cannot do much. Enclosed you will find my little mite and I will pray that you may be able to keep on the air.

A lady writes from the mid-west: I am praying for my relatives who are unsaved. My neighbor, who was a terrible drunkard, has been gloriously saved through listening to your sermon on "The Woman at the Well."

From Washington State: I have had a real soul struggle since early last winter and could not find any promise of forgiveness for years of wilfully neglecting Christ, in spite of the fact that I have known the truth since I was a child. I could make a long story of my wilful sins, but, thanks be to God, I came to the light last Sunday night while listening to your sermon. I am shouting within my soul, glory to His name.

Dear Mr. Fuller: As you closed your meeting Sunday night, I got down on my knees by the radio and prayed that I would be forgiven. I once knew what it was to have peace with God and it seemed so hard to come back. But I do praise Him, this morning, that I stayed home Sunday evening and listened to your sermon. You made it plain, and now I am back in the fold.

From just two broadcasts: After the broadcast, last Sunday, it was my intention to follow the Master. Somehow, though, there was something lacking. Tonight's message was a true answer to prayer. It is hard to explain, but I was trying to follow under my own strength. How you have made it clear! If in two broadcasts you could show me the light so plainly, for which I have been searching for years, what a glorious work must be going on in other homes and hearts.

Dear Mr. Fuller: Your messages about prophecy have, to my personal knowledge, led a father, a son and a daughter-in-law to a saving knowledge of Christ. These people are my closest neighbors, and since their conversion I've been helping them search the Scriptures, using my Scofield Reference Bible.

A man writes from Canada: We can assure you that your work is of great blessing for I found the Lord Jesus through the radio sermon just two weeks ago tonight. I feel like a different person; my sins are forgiven. My wife and I want to devote the rest of our lives to the service of Christ.

A lady writes from Washington: I cannot find words to tell you the blessings I receive from the Old Fashioned Revival Hour. When I tell you how utterly miserable I was until the Sunday night of August 27th and then how our heavenly Father gave you the message that has changed my whole life into one of joy and peace that satisfied my every longing, you will understand the words aren't made to describe my feeling.

A sent-one: We're so thankful for the Old Fashioned Revival Hour. A friend of ours was finally saved through hearing you over the radio. She is oh so happy and goes everywhere she can telling the story of Jesus' love.

The hired man listens, too: I was converted many years ago and used to attend church regularly. But after coming out here to a small town I just about starved out spiritually, until I found I could get good sermons over the radio. I discovered your program a few months ago. It is just what we need. Several times we have asked our hired man over to listen in on your program, and one Sunday evening, about five weeks ago, after you had given the call, he said that if he was down there where you were he would go to the altar. I suggested he make his altar right here in our home and he did, and was gloriously saved.

A young lady in Massachusetts writes: I wish to tell you that I was born again on October 15th, the night of your broadcast on the Roman Empire. As I was listening to your sermon I suddenly began to realize that I was lost, and I felt as though there was some great warning for me in your sermon. I have found calm and peace in my life since then.

From Seattle: A few weeks ago we received into our church, by baptism, a tall, fine looking young man who told us that he was saved through listening to the Old Fashioned Revival Hour. Wife and I are both past seventy, and it's such a blessing to us that we can sit in our home and be blessed in our souls before we go to our church for the evening service.

A lady writes from Florida: My husband was saved three weeks ago, right after your program. We knelt down and prayed and he gave his heart to God here in our home. I can't praise Him enough for His goodness in answering our prayers. My husband is sixty-three years old.

Good news from Idaho: I have some good news to tell you! A little while ago I was visiting some of my dear friends. The father of the family, whom I had not seen for some time, happened to be there that day. He is almost eighty years old. All his life he has been very sinful, drinking whiskey, hating people, and committing many other sins. That day, as he and I were talking, I could tell from his talk that he was a changed man. I said to him, "Dad, have you had a change of heart; have you been saved?"

"Well," he said, "I'll tell you. About a year ago I picked up a little folder that you had left here at the house telling of the Charles Fuller broadcast. I got to listening to him and I was saved. I don't see how anybody could listen to him preaching a year and not be saved. I used to be such a drunkard and craved whiskey, but now God has taken that craving all away. I am a different man altogether now, and I am happy." And I can tell he is a different man from talking to him.

A lady from Colorado writes: We have three members of one family who have just been received into our B. Y. P. U. who were converted by listening to your broadcast. It is wonderful how they have strengthened our Union and have been such a blessing to our church.

A thirst for God's Word created: We wanted to write and tell you how that, through your broadcast, my wife and I were saved. In our humble way we can't thank you enough for your messages that tell of a Redeemer who can win sinners. The best time we ever had was when God poured His blessing on us and gave us a thirst for the things of His Word. He took away worldly desires out of our hearts and brought love for our fellow men in. He also took my tobacco habit away instantly. Glory to His name!

A California listener has a spiritual awakening: I would be most ungrateful were I not to give thanks to God for causing me to turn my radio dial to KNX in order that I might listen to your wonderful message. It brought forth in me an awakening that I never experienced before—a spiritual awakening. I have slipped terribly during the past two years, but I sincerely hope that I now have the courage and strength to turn completely away from sin and put my absolute trust in God. I sincerely thank you, from the bottom of my heart, for what your messages have done for me.

Another California letter: My dear little mother, who is ninety-four years old, lives in Colorado. She has been hearing your wonderful programs for four years and she asked me if I would not tune in so that we would be closer together—at least it would seem so. I did so, three weeks ago, and oh, you don't know the joy I have received from your old songs. They make me cry, for they are the ones Mother sang about her work, God bless her, when I was a child at home. It was through a bitter experience that I came to the feet of God, and now I feel I can never repay Christ for His sacrificial death for me.

"I have just sinned too much": Your sermon, tonight, on the Woman at the Well was so clear that I could grasp the truth, and I now accept and receive Christ as my personal Saviour. So long I have been trying to get to the Lord and just this morning I thought, "Well, I hate to be lost, but I guess I will have to give up because I have just sinned too much." I am so glad I heard that sermon, and I thank God for making a way of escape for a sinner.

A wife prayed thirteen years for this husband: My dearest brother in Christ:—Yes, I mean that, for by God's grace and through your ministry over the air I have been brought to that place where I can call Him my heavenly Father and His Son my Saviour. Oh, I thank and praise the Lord for that day, nearly two and a half years ago, when you said, "You, there by your radio, why don't you raise your hand and accept the Lord Jesus and say, 'Lord Jesus, come into my heart.'" I could not keep my hand down and have thanked the Lord ever since for saving me, an unworthy sinner. My wife had been praying for me for thirteen years and my mother for thirty-six years. Prayer changes things. We have four children, and three have now accepted the Lord Jesus and we have all been baptized and rejoice in what the Lord has done for us.

From a four weeks' old Christian in British Columbia: I have listened to three of your talks and I am glad to say that they have led me to Jesus. By the time you read this I will be four weeks old in my new life. Christ has led me by the hand and no one can pluck me out. What a feeling of safety!

This New Mexican woman found that trying wasn't enough: I want to thank you for the sermon that you preached, last Sunday night. My husband and I enjoyed it so much. After hearing you my husband just dropped down, then and there, in front of our radio, and gave himself into God's safe keeping. Oh, you will never know how happy it made me. I can never thank you enough for bringing that message to us away up here in the mountains where we hardly ever hear a sermon preached except by radio. I have tried for some time to live a Christian life, but I see now that this isn't enough. I want to try to help win others for Christ, so I think I will invite a crowd for Sunday afternoon to start a kind of Bible class and then listen in.

Saved, and attending church: I think it is proper that I should write and tell you of two happy changes in our family since we started listening to your program, this fall. My wife and I, aged twenty-six and twenty-seven, were saved two weeks ago. It was largely through hearing the splendid sermons by you. It resulted in our attending a church which preaches the true gospel. I have not stopped praising the Lord for bringing us both at the same time.

This young couple in Oregon have no other opportunity to hear the gospel: Praise God, our home is now a Christian one since my husband gave his heart to Christ after listening to your sermon on January 30th. We had listened regularly for a month or more. I had been praying earnestly for him. The radio is our only means of hearing God's Word preached, as we live way out in the country and have no car. We are both twenty-four years of age and have been married only eight months. We are anxious to travel the narrow way through life, the way that leads to a home in Heaven.

From Iowa—burdened with worry and trouble: While listening to your broadcast on January 29th, I was converted, thank God! Your sermon touched me and when you said you felt constrained to make mention of young men who were burdened with worry and trouble I felt that God Himself had put those words into your mouth for me. I am twenty years old, and it was the first time I had ever heard your broadcast. Frequently, during the past few months, I felt I did not care much about living, but since I have been saved I see everything different.

This woman found joy after making things right: I can sing and praise God's holy name, this Monday morning, because I opened my heart to Him last Sunday night during your message. I have had so many things to make right that I have said against the dearest ones that I have on earth. As I write this, my heart is so much lighter, as I have gone and made restitution for the wrongs I have done. I can never tell you how happy I am to be rid of the load of sin and to know that I have done everything I can to make things right with others.

This Long Island man was sinking into sin: I have been listening to your radio broadcasts for three weeks. I must just tell you what a blessing they have been to me. For the past year I have been unemployed. Due to my great hardship and discouragement I have allowed myself to slip away on the path of Satan. I was sinking into sin very rapidly until three weeks ago. While very much burdened and discouraged, I turned on my radio and heard your program. Last Sunday night, after listening, I just knelt down and gave myself to God, upon hearing your invitation. Now I am so happy again.

From a hospital in Detroit: Last Sunday night, I heard your program again and how my soul was refreshed. It was a year ago last October, while I was listening to your program, that I was converted. You used the verse, "Him that cometh unto me I will in no wise cast out." Many, many a time I have heard that verse quoted in sermons, but somehow that time it seemed just for me. I just simply believed that if I came humbly God would receive me, and He did. Right after I was converted I was admitted as a tubercular patient to this hospital and have been here over a year. I have never forgotten that day when I came to Christ, and I have never ceased to pray for you.

From a school teacher in Montana: You probably don't remember, but I am one who was converted while listening last winter. I wrote and told you how hungry I was for the Word and asked you to pray for Mother and Dad that they, too, might be saved. Well, praise the Lord, tonight my daddy was saved. Isn't it glorious how God answers prayer. I am so happy that I want to shout and sing. The path of a Christian is not an easy one, but it is a glorious, satisfying, safe path. I am glad that at least three of our family are treading it now.

From a Mississippi listener: I listen to the Old Fashioned Revival Hour every Sunday night. I can hardly wait until the next Sunday. I love to hear you preach, as you make it so plain. I have wanted to become a Christian for a long time, but I live two miles from town and have five small children, so I haven't been going to church. I heard your sermon, last Sunday night, and after that I just could not wait any longer. I knelt right in front of my radio and gave myself to Christ. He has wonderfully saved me. My husband had been without work for some time. Everything looked so hopeless before, but now such peace and joy have come to me.

From San Francisco: I never miss one of your broadcasts and I want to tell you that through them I have found God. I never could tell you what a wonderful change it has made in my life. I just wish I could have understood this years ago. I feel as though all my past life has been wasted. I shall always thank God that you have made things so plain for me that I have never understood before.

A new man in Christ Jesus: We have been praying, for a long time, for the conversion of a man here who did not attend church. A few Sundays ago he came to church and gave his testimony, saying that he had been converted by listening to the Old Fashioned Revival Hour and that he is now a new man in Christ Jesus.

This man made a great discovery: We have good news for you tonight. My dear husband, after your message on Sunday night, gave his heart to Christ as simply and humbly as a little child. He said in his prayer, "God, be merciful to me and forgive me. I accept Thee with all my heart and believe Thy Word." Yes, my husband, who had gotten off into great darkness and unbelief has come back. He ridiculed God's Word and ridiculed you, Mr. Fuller. Oh, what the Enemy can get men to do and say. But your messages from the Word, prayers, and songs have reached a hard, scoffing, bitter, old man and have brought him back to the foot of the cross. How thankful we are.

A blind lady in Omaha writes, on a typewriter: I want to tell you that my brother accepted Christ through listening to your broadcast and he's a changed man. He has given up drinking, also smoking. It surely is wonderful how God works with those who have gone so many years in this life without Christ. He is fifty years old.

A Georgia song of praise: I want to write and tell you that my husband and I tune in the minute you all come on the air. My husband has to walk on a peg leg, and we would have to walk five miles to church, so we stay at home. My husband has been converted and learned to love the Lord from hearing you all over the radio, and we just tell everybody to tune in and hear you all. How we do love the song, "Meet Me There," for we have two little children that have gone on to the glory land, and other loved ones. We just can't miss hearing every bit of your program, because it means so much to us and comforts us. We would also be glad to get your picture and would like to meet you all. You know when a husband gets converted it means lots to us mothers.

From British Columbia: Earlier in the year I wrote and asked if there was any hope for a wayward and sinful girl, and your reply was that there was all the hope in Christ Jesus for me. Well, last night, it all came true in answer to your prayers, for I gave my heart to Him and now I am one of His children. It has been a hard and bitter struggle, but, thank God, it is over. Will you remember me in your prayers and ask God to strengthen my faith, for I am still weak and there are many barriers to overcome. I sincerely thank you for your letter and tracts, and I can assure you that they have been read, many times. May God richly bless you for showing me the plain, simple way of salvation.

Kansans stirred by a message on the times in which we live: My husband and I listen to your program every Sunday and we are glad that we have this opportunity. The Sunday that you gave the message concerning the alliance between Russia and Germany we came to thinking exactly what great sinners we were and, that night, we both gave our hearts to Christ. We are a happy pair now.

From Chicago: We have been hearing the Old Fashioned Revival Hour for the past two years and it is through your plain teaching of God's Word that our whole family has accepted Christ as our Saviour. We were all baptized on June 18, as you advised, and it was a wonderful experience. When I stood in the water waiting my turn I just knew that Christ was there with me.

A young man, too: I am a young man of twenty-one, and have been listening all winter to your broadcast, as I have been taking care of a bed-ridden, elderly man on Sundays while his family got out a little. My home is not a Christian one and I have had no Christian training or influence. I wondered why this old man always wanted me to turn the radio on so early, for fear he would miss a part of your program. As I listened, I began to be interested and realized my need of a Saviour. You have made the way of salvation so clear that I want you to know I have accepted Christ as my Saviour. I want to learn more of the Bible and I want to serve Christ.

A lady writes a lovely letter from Iowa: I'm writing to tell you how thankful I am for the broadcast. We have listened for a long time. At first there were two of us, my husband and I, but over eight months ago he went Home, a saved man because of your broadcast. He accepted Christ as he listened to the messages over the radio.

From Washington State: We enjoy the Old Fashioned Revival Hour as much as anything on the air. My husband has been saved in our home since listening to you. I love the way you preach the Word of God. We sit with our Bible and follow you. Our home is a changed place since Christ has come here to stay. You wouldn't believe it!

A backslider reclaimed: We are rather aged people and live in the country, with no car, no church near by, so you have become part of our very lives. The other night, having been sick in bed for some time and quite discouraged, I just turned on the radio to find something and the Old Fashioned Revival Hour came on. Through listening I have again found my Saviour and I am so happy about it that I want to shout it to all the world. I was converted when I was a child but as the years went on I drifted away from God. Now I have come back.

From a far away northern town: I cannot begin to tell you how much I have learned about the Bible from your broadcasts. I never really understood God's wonderful plan of salvation through Christ Jesus until I heard you explain it over the radio. When I did I knelt there and prayed. That was almost a year ago. I think I must have felt like Atlas with the world lifted off his back, only my world was of self and sin. I can never thank you enough for helping me find Christ.

A regular church member, but not saved: I was a regular church member but, last night, I just happened to tune in to the Old Fashioned Revival Hour and I wish to tell you how wonderfully I was blessed by the songs and also the message. I was deep in sin, but God spoke to my heart as I listened to your program. With tears streaming down my face I knelt by the side of my bed and gave my heart to Christ, asking for forgiveness.

A backslider in Alabama came back to God: I received a very special blessing tonight from listening to you. I praise and thank God for His goodness to me. I was a backslider. For weeks I have wanted to come back to God, but I thought there was no hope for me. Tonight, praise God, while listening to your broadcast I heard you say, while you were preaching, that you felt there was some soul in radio-land whose heart was heavy and who needed God. Those words went to my heart and I knew they were meant for me. Conviction seized my soul and I dropped to my knees and prayed for forgiveness. The burden rolled off my heart and I am free again.

This woman asked for bread and was given a stone: I heard a part of your radio message in which you were appealing for those outside of Christ. It brought me under deep conviction, and I went to a nearby minister for help. I came away as troubled as I went, for he had nothing to offer me. Again, next Sunday, I turned in to the broadcast. The way of salvation was made plain and I accepted Christ. I am glad to witness to His saving grace.

From a weary wayfarer: A few weeks ago I listened to your Revival Hour for the first time. The old fashioned hymns took me back to childhood days and the little church and Sunday school. For many years I have been a wanderer, far from the old teachings. But your sermon and your hymns brought me back again. I gave my heart to God, that night, and asked Him to take a weary wayfarer back into the fold.

A drunkard reclaimed: I wrote you in October, 1936, asking prayer for my unsaved husband who drank terribly. In your reply you said to me, "Write us when you have the answer." Thank God, I do have the answer now. My husband was saved a week ago yesterday, and that craving for drink has all been taken away from him. Truly, he is a new creature in Christ Jesus. We know it is God that has done this in answer to prayer, and are humbly thankful. I pray for your broadcasts and will help when I can.

A brother saved, too: I have the great satisfaction of telling you that after your broadcast of Sunday night, April 3rd, my brother called us by long distance and said he and his wife had started to live the Christian life, and they were saved while listening to your message that night. We are unable to express our gratitude to God for such wonderful results from the Old Fashioned Revival Hour.

13

TOUCHING EVERY AREA OF HUMAN NEED

THE MANNER in which the Old Fashioned Revival
Hour reaches out into every area of life and influ-
ences those who hear its message is illustrated by the following letters. One is made to realize, as one reads hundreds of these letters, how unlimited by location, voca-
tion, nationality or creed is the vast audience reached.

From a movie actress in Hollywood: I am a motion picture actress. You have reached out to people in every walk
of life, and I just wanted you to know that you have at
least one well-wisher and firm believer in all you preach in
the film colony. I have told many of my picture friends to
listen to your broadcast. I try, on every picture that I
work on, to mention something about the Lord, the times
we are living in, that God's prophecies are being fulfilled,
and that the time is short.

From an unemployed laborer in Ohio: As I have listened
to your programs over the air I have found the Lord as my
Saviour. I have been laid off my job and things look dingy
to me, but if we let down when the way gets hard we

amount to nothing, because anyone can serve God when everything is going good.

A Jew listens in: I heard your broadcast, Sunday night, and I enjoyed it very much. Such programs as yours is what America needs in these days, to offset the doctrines of hatred. May the great God bless and continue the Old Fashioned Revival Hour. I am a Jew, and it is heartrending to note that two men who claim to be servants and ministers of God are doing much damage to the Jewish people in America by their spread of anti-semitism. May the God of Moses be with you. (Signed, "From a Jew of the Jewish Orthodox faith")

From the Dust Bowl: This is intended to be a Christmas greeting to you and the rest of the Hour folks. There are thousands of folks just like us who sit in their loneliness, as we do here in our "dust bowl" (and let me say, it is a real dust bowl) and listen to the broadcast with the eagerness of hungry men looking for food. Tears trickle down our cheeks when the strains of the much-loved songs reach our ears. Our hearts leap for joy when the precious Word is read and expounded and prayers are lifted to the Father above for *every* listener, and that includes us. And we think of the many who have never accepted Jesus, whose hearts fear lest it is too late, and pray that the word of guidance may be given them and that they, too, may know the Word and accept Christ. When sinners are told to quietly kneel by their radio and say, "Here I am; save me, for Jesus' sake," I know how it feels and what it means because I have had the experience of doing that. Keep right on telling it. There are thousands of church people who are glad to hear that message, for their church going has not given them assurance. May everyone who has given for the support of the Hour know that something more precious than money is "harvested."

From a woman in jail in Arkansas: What happy people you two must be. What glorious work you are doing. I have been in jail eight months and have been saved only seven months. How your program feeds my starved soul. It seems my cell is filled with the Spirit of God when I hear the Old Fashioned Revival every Sunday evening. Tonight I received such a blessing from your program in Boston that I had to write and tell you.

Miners in Nevada: I heard you way out in the hills of Nevada, last Sunday, about sixty miles from the nearest church. The whole crew of miners listened attentively. I do not believe that any of them would have gone to church if they had had the chance. Your broadcast reaches people that the churches cannot.

An Indian woman is converted: An Indian woman, some time ago, heard your message over the radio. It touched her heart so much she began to inquire about how to get religion. She kept listening to your messages faithfully, despite the difficulties of abuse and scoffing of her family and Indian relatives. Finally the truth entered her heart and she became thoroughly converted by your messages. She immediately set out to save her family and relatives. She has been so successful that all of them are converted except her old Indian chief father. He is under conviction but has not yet taken his stand. Now, this Indian woman and all of her children are dying of "Indian consumption" and are all suffering much in the last stages, in their crowded shack, lonely, neglected, merely existing. But despite this suffering the smile of joy shines upon all their faces. They know they have not long to live, but they are ready to go to be with their precious Lord.

A disabled war veteran writes from Kansas: I am writing to you to let you know what a blessing we get out of hearing you folks. It has been the cause of me and my wife getting back to the Lord. Up until about six weeks ago I was an awful drunkard. I have not touched a drop since the Lord saved me. You folks are doing a wonderful work. I am a disabled war veteran.

A nurse sends in a contribution: Herewith is one dollar to help boost the radio work. I am a nurse, and this very bill came from our "red light" district where I nursed last night and shall again tonight. My poor little patient is thirty-two, a former "Follies dancer,"—T. B., dope addict, in convulsions, has five sisters who "mill around" the bed (several so drunk I tactfully sent them away). Of course I talked to them of the way of salvation and, tonight, shall take some tracts. I plead your prayers for them, that they will accept before it is too late. A "tramp" who recently cleaned my yard said your radio programs were always such a blessing to him. God bless you spiritually and temporally.

From Illinois: I just listened to your broadcast and it's the best I ever heard. I do not know how we could live through the week if we could not sit at Christ's table and feast on your sermons, for life is so hard. I have seven children, four of them are stepchildren. Their father was killed. I'm trying so hard to raise them right. I love to see them sit by the radio, when you are preaching, and drink it in.

THE SHEEP ARE FED

While the appeal is particularly to the unsaved in every broadcast, the immense encouragement and enlightenment which comes to thousands of Christians must not be overlooked. The creeping paralysis of apostasy in The Church has undoubtedly produced a feeling of deep pessimism in the hearts of many believers who wonder whether Faith will be found on the earth if the spiritual slump continues. What a joy to witness the power of the gospel at work in the lives of men and women! What a blessing in gathering around the Word with millions of others in the great circle of God's family! Here are some heart warming letters:

Tragedy of loneliness and longing: Once more your blessed service has ended, giving me again the courage to go on and leave my burdens with the Lord. Your wonderful singers sang, tonight, "Home of the Soul," which always brings my precious mother, who went to this Home only a few weeks ago, so near to me. At the same time, my own problems, heartaches and loneliness crowded in on me until I was almost overcome with grief and despair. Then those wonderful voices started singing, as it were right to me, that wonderful song, "Never Give Up." It came to me as though sent from God, as I believe it was. Before I had time to more than grasp this song, as a drowning person might a rope, you came with that message of faith, "At Thy word, Lord." God bless these meetings is all I can say. If you knew the tragedy of loneliness and longing that is in our home now you might more fully realize what your blessed Hour means in our lives.

Dear Mr. Fuller: Myself and my husband have been listening to your program over a year and I'm ashamed that I haven't written before to tell you how much it means to an elderly couple. My husband is an invalid and cannot get out and cannot read very much, so the radio means so much to him, as we look forward all week to your Hour. A few weeks ago you sang, "Close to Thee," and it has gone with me all the weeks since as a prayer and has comforted me when the way has seemed hard. We live on the farm where my husband was born and, although he can no longer do anything to keep it up, it still seems more like home to him than any other place could. So we're trying to stay here. We have a few hens, a garden, three cows and two pigs, so make our living that way. I had hoped to send you something before this to help with the work that we love so much and that helps other lonely people like ourselves to be comforted. I have sold some chickens recently so am sending a little to help in getting on your larger hook-up. I have told quite a few people about your broadcast, but it seems as though all of them already listen in and think as much of it as we do.

How Christians need to have clean hearts: I am a girl of twenty-one and have been saved a year and a half. Before that great change took place in my life I was a church member but not a regenerated one. Several months ago, at a consecration service, I raised my hand to signify that I wanted to give my life to the Lord. Tonight, though, while listening to your program, the Spirit seemed to speak right to me and I wanted to be able to say from the bottom of my heart, "Lord, cleanse me from everything that would hinder my being used as a vessel for Thee." After the message was over I re-dedicated my life for God's service.

A good letter from New York: I read the article you referred to, last night, that rural churches are disappearing at the rate of one thousand per year. The writer doesn't seem to touch the real core of the matter as to why the churches are empty. For about six years now I have been going to church hungry and going home hungry. Very little gospel or Bible do we hear and never a word on the Lord's return. We have a play, musical, pictures, anything to get the people out. Out to what? If they want those things, the playhouse is across the street. There is no substitute for the simple gospel given in the power of the Holy Spirit. No, starved children cannot grow. Empty tables are not attractive.

What would we do without these true-to-the-Word messages which you give.

A wonderful testimony from Georgia: As the sleet and snow were pouring down, last Sunday evening, it prevented me from attending church services. Turning the dial on the radio I was asking God that I might hear a service on this Lord's Day and though it was so many miles away yours came in so clearly and was such a blessing to me. You certainly are doing a wonderful work out there in California. I have been living for Christ now for the past three years and I get such peace and happiness out of my faith. I am the mother of four children who are lost. My husband is a drunkard. My mother lives with me. She is eighty-four years old and has been bedridden for three years. I don't know what I would do without Christ. He strengthens me when I am weak; He makes the darkest hours bright; He is my all.

From California: I was saved nearly two years ago, after an auto accident which nearly cost my life, but I backslid and went the way of the world. Your messages which I have hungrily absorbed have brought me back to the Lord. And now "He Keeps Me Singing." Praise His Name. I take notes on your sermons, and portions of them remain in my heart. I am studying the Bible, for I feel that God saved me from death to serve Him completely and to be a real testimony for Him in this valley, for there are few Christians here. I am a young mother of five children and was deep in sin. Each Saturday night found me in a ball room. All the money I could lay hands on was spent for clothes for parties and dances. I drank, smoked, and served the devil well. And now I am glad to tell my former associates of Jesus.

From Alberta, Canada: We, my husband and I, are engaged in mission work out here in Canada's needy prairie. Last Sunday, we had the joy of hearing one of your broadcasts. Our hearts were blessed and refreshed and filled with gratitude to him for the sound preaching of the Word over the air.

From Indiana, a lady writes: I beg to state that we are tired of modern oratorical sermons and we are just hungering for the old time gospel sermons. I stumbled on yours, one night, and was so delighted with it. We long for it to come on every week and can hardly wait. It revives us in our faith. We have gotten many others to listen in and they are all well pleased.

A church official in Philadelphia who occupies one of the pews of the nation wide audience: We have listened with delight and I have, for some time, regretted that the day of the great revivalists, like Moody, Billy Sunday, Torrey and Chapman seem to have passed away. The church is showing a lack of it, as they not only reached the unsaved but built up those who had already named the name of Christ. Perhaps this new age needs new methods for proclaiming the grand old gospel. The masses will be reached by this method of the radio broadcast that you are using. May God give you physical and spiritual strength to continue.

A man from Houston, Texas, writes: I wish to report that on your "Tell Another" week I contacted and told over two hundred people about your broadcast, giving the radio logs to many of them. Of course I met a few scoffers, but most of those I contacted were glad to hear about the program, though some already knew about it. It certainly is soul food to a Christian and a life buoy to the lost. Please send me another hundred logs, as there are several people waiting for them.

GOSPEL MUSIC HAS A LARGE PART IN WINNING SOULS

Unquestionably the familiar old gospel songs used in Mr. Fuller's broadcast are exerting a powerful influence over his listeners. To many of these, the songs recall childhood days, praying fathers and mothers, and the little church in some far away country town from which they have drifted during many years. The following letters are typical.

He joined the choir: Following your last evening's suggestion I am writing you, this morning, to tell you how much I appreciated your service last evening. I am an old man, nearing my eighty-third milestone. My hearing has gotten so bad that I seldom go to the evening church service. My wife and I live alone, as our children are all in homes of their own. I insist on my wife going to church even if I do not go. Last evening I seemed to be unusually lonesome, so I tried the radio, and I discovered you people were singing the good old songs which used to thrill me in my own church and Sunday school years ago. I want to tell you how much I enjoyed that singing. I could hear and understand every word and, when they started singing, "What a Friend We Have in Jesus," I could not keep quiet. I started in on the bass just as I used to do years ago. I really felt that the other singers were near me and such a thrill I have not had for years! After the singing I enjoyed your message of a sin-free conscience. I realize that I am a back number in modern church activities. I do not enjoy the modern, so-called solos which no one understands. I say, "Let all the people sing."

They fill a real need: I had the privilege of hearing you last Sunday evening. We took a trip out into the country, Sunday, and on our way home we stopped to listen to the Old Fashioned Revival Hour over the radio in our car. I so seldom get a chance to listen in that I enjoyed it more than ever. I especially enjoyed the singing of the young people.

The choruses are what I like. I certainly wish more ministers realized how people hunger for gospel music, and not the classical type that is beyond the average listener's appreciation of music. I am so thankful for the few gospel programs that are on the radio, for they fill a great need. I think we Christian people should be especially thankful for those who are faithful in witnessing right down the devil's lane (the air lane).

The whole nation goes to church when the Old Fashioned Revival Hour goes on the air. It is probable that the listening audience to this service is equal to the audiences of all the Sunday evening church services in the nation. Its appeal to millions who have lost interest in the church has an astounding significance. It has demonstrated, more than any other event of the past decade, that a great number of people are still interested in Christianity if they can have the simple gospel truths which in too many cases are not being heard in the churches of our nation.

The old fashioned methods had their advantages: I have concluded that the modern idea of not singing our children to sleep must have been a trick of Satan. The memory of the dear old hymns my mother sang to me and which we children of our large family later sang together is the most lasting and happy family memory to me. My mother was wonderfully saved at the age of sixteen and, though in later years two of her sons were laid away and our home and all we had was burned within a year, that did not hinder her from singing hymns of praise to God. These memories, quickened by your Old Fashioned Revival Hour, are a great joy in these troubled times. Thank you, and God grant that you may continue as long as your strength endures. Your program comes through to the east coast as clear as local stations, and I wish it came more often.

14

THE BRINK OF SUICIDE

Suicides have often been prevented in the nick of time by the message of hope preached by Mr. Fuller, as these letters testify.

The message pierced the darkness: Tonight, as I sat in the darkness of despair, with my radio tuned on nothing special, your message of "Who then can be saved?" came to me. Oh, how it helped me. I was just planning how I could get out of this life in the quickest way—a terrible thought—but I have just been left all alone and it seemed I could not stand it. Thanks a million times for your message. It came so clearly to me through the dark, piercing my darkness. I hope to continue to get a great deal out of your sermons. "Lord, I come to Thee."

The bitterness melted when this person found Christ: God's answer to prayer in my behalf is so unbelievable to any but a Christian that I sometimes stand amazed myself. Last fall I had a serious nervous breakdown after surgery and attempted suicide. A few days before I had written Mr. Fuller in absolute desperation, hoping the prayers of the prayer warriors might save me from such a fearful act. Truly someone was praying because, although I took a large quantity of poison, my life was saved. It was just a few days later that Mr. Fuller's letter came. Somehow the bitterness melted from my heart and I truly learned to take my burden to the Lord and leave it there. Since then I have found remarkable blessing. I am almost well and attending school. Our financial situation is very serious. I am trying so hard to be brave and wait on the Lord. Sometimes my courage nearly fails. It is then that I get out Mr. Fuller's old letter and read and reread his promise, "We shall continue to bear you up definitely in prayer until you have full victory and peace in Christ."

The revolver was at his head: I have been out of the navy for a year and am twenty-four years old. Work has been so scarce that I have been forced to work in a beer garden. At the rear of the beer garden is my room, and I happened to win a radio on a punch board. When it is time for your broadcast, I just slip out and listen. I have been saved by hearing the broadcasts. I went to your service in the Olympia out of curiosity. I have been a terrible sinner.

How I have changed! My friends cannot realize that I am the same person. I am happy and so relieved of all these burdens. A young chap was in the beer garden the other Sunday. He seemed so despondent. I followed him to the lavatory and found him just pressing a revolver to his head. I knocked it out of his hand and took him to my room. We had been there only ten minutes when your gospel Hour came. He sat there amazed at hearing those wonderful songs and that beautiful piano playing. I must be short—so he was saved—yes, saved by hearing the broadcast. In four weeks I have had three more conversions. Would like suggestions how to carry on. Should I quit this job or not?

An unsigned letter from a desperate young woman: Do

you know that the old songs you sing on the radio were the lullabys with which my mother sang me to sleep when I was a little girl? Yes, I had a Christian mother. Thank God, she is in Heaven tonight and does not know the truth about me. Does anyone become so vile that the Lord cannot save her? Is there any hope for me, as far down as I am?

A letter from Washington: I have been listening to your program since last January. My husband was instantly killed on January 11. At that time I was deep in sin. I said to my mother, "Is there a just God?" Mother said, "Yes, God knows best. There is always a silver lining." If it had not been for praying parents and your broadcast I am afraid I would have ended it all, I suffered so. But I was saved by listening to your broadcast the 27th day of March. I am so happy in Christ now and am looking for Him to come soon.

Marital trouble, a common cause of despair: I am so thankful for the Old Fashioned Revival Hour. I would not have seen this new year if it hadn't been for your program. Some weeks ago I returned home, one Sunday morning, from a distant city where I had been seeking employment. While I had been gone that week I had been thinking of my every day life and I knew that I was backslidden and trying to go on in this troubled world without including God.

On returning to the house, Sunday, I found a letter addressed to me saying that my wife had left and had taken the babies with her. I was so shocked when I read it; it made me frantic. I cared very much for my family, though in thinking things over I knew that I could have been more kind and considerate. I drove hastily to her mother's home, where my wife had gone, and begged her to come back but she would not, and I returned home without her and the babies. Simply grief stricken, I did not care to go on living without my wife.

166

That evening I decided I couldn't stand it and decided to end it all. The future looked so dark, and I couldn't go on alone. I went into the garage and closed the doors tight and started the car motor and turned on the radio. I lay down under the back of the car and, in a short time, I began to feel my head thumping and felt myself slowly going out from this life and I did not care. I felt that I wished it would work quicker. The radio was going, and it sounded like a loud racket as my head roared and boomed like a jungle drum. I hoped all would soon be over. Then I heard a powerful voice speak again and it was speaking to God in prayer. As I heard Mr. Fuller praying I began to realize what was really happening. I knew I was not ready to go and was fearful of what the future might hold. I gathered my strength and crawled as a helpless creature to the door. How I got it open I do not know. I shudder when I think how near I came to eternity and hell. I didn't talk to God even then but He was surely watching over me. In the days that followed I couldn't eat, I couldn't sleep, and I felt I had to choose between God and Satan, but I couldn't bear my cross. I wanted to get away from it all.

A short time afterward I drove a thousand miles or more, to get away from this place that had been so dear to me, but when I arrived there I wanted to go right back. I had gone over a week without sleep, and I had eaten very little. I fell unconscious at the wheel in a distant city and it has been a round of hospitals and jails since then. But I have come back to God. I am at home again. My mother and father have been so kind. This new year finds me at church praying to God as I have never prayed before, and I am beginning to get my health and strength back.

I have not been able to see my family as yet, but am looking forward and praying for the day when we will all be together again as a happy family. I am now trusting God and

I wonder how we could endure without Him and His wonderful Word, in times of trial and sore trouble. I do thank Him for this program which strengthens us in the faith.

From Pittsburgh, Penna: It is now past midnight in my home and I have been listening to your program. I am glad to say your message in song and sermon has changed my life from a young man ready to commit suicide to a young man praying that he may find work. I am twenty-three years old and have been out of work eight months. I was told Thursday that if I didn't pay my rent by the 25th of the month I would be put out of the house, so you can see why I felt as I did, but the Lord is going to take care of me now, I am confident of that. I would like to have the map of stations which you plan to use starting in September, and I hope one of them is in Pittsburgh. May God bless you and keep your program on the air. (Signed, "One of the sinners you have brought to Christ")

Under Conviction of Sin

Many letters are received from those who are deeply under conviction, but have not yet been saved. These letters are a matter of particular concern to Mr. and Mrs. Fuller and their associates, who try by every means to bring them to a place of real surrender. Personal letters are written, tracts and other helpful literature are sent and much time is spent in intercessory prayer for them. A few samples of such letters are given, herewith.

From Portland, Oregon: I tuned my radio and heard singing. Later I heard you preach, and I believe that God was in it that I heard the program. I am a poor, lost sinner; a wicked sinner. My mother said, "My boy, when will you turn to God."

I said, "I will before long."

Just before Mother died I promised her I would come soon. My parents were Christians. I have spurned the Holy Spirit so much and now I can't get through. I sought God for years but did not find Him, and was ready to give up all, but I heard your program. Will you please pray for me that the Holy Spirit may convict me but once more. Please pray for me. I haven't the clothes to go to church or even a rescue mission. God well knows that I want to pray through. I have been in jail twice. Oh, pray! Please, please, please.

From Tennessee: I am a night watchman at a mining camp. I have a little radio here and have been listening to your service for quite a while. I sure enjoy it. I was once a Christian and I want you to pray for me that God will take me back again.

The following comes from a sin-burdened woman in San Francisco: I am only a sinner. I can't even write good in English, but I want you to pray for me and ask the Lord to help me be a good woman. I am a very bad woman. I hope you will pray for me.

Here is a sad letter from South Dakota: For a long time I have wanted to write you but didn't do it. Today I just have to do it. I am a sick woman, suffering from tuberculosis for more than two years in a South Dakota sanatorium. I sometimes despair even of life to know that I cannot see my dear little ones and be with them just when they need me most. I was left alone to face this cruel world with my little ones. The worst of everything is to know that I am lost, without Christ. I am not a Christian yet and I ask your help, as I don't wish anything on earth but to return to Christ. I know myself lost without Him and wandering in a strange country. Won't you ask your audience to pray for me? I want most to accept Christ and next I ask for my health so I can once more be with my little ones who need me so badly.

From a California listener: When you asked for those to raise their hands who wished from now on to have our Saviour Jesus for their own personal Saviour I raised mine high even though I was of the unseen radio audience. I do wish this with all my heart. However, I have lived a terrible life. Will you and your dear wife offer up a prayer for me. Ask God to forgive my many sins and give me strength.

A touching letter from Canada: I have heard your broadcasts on Sunday evenings. I used to go to church and took an active part in things, but I committed a terrible sin against God and against myself, not realizing what I was doing, although I should have. It has affected both my mind and body to such an extent that I know no rest day or night. When I hear you speak so happily it just condemns me. Is there forgiveness for me? I just feel that God's Spirit has left me. It is dreadful for my husband and family who have done so much for me. What is the unforgiveable sin? I fear I have committed it. I see no hope for me here or in the world to come. Please pray for me. (Signed, "A woman in absolute despair")

A young woman in Alberta, Canada: About six months ago my dear mother, who is a real Christian, was listening on the crystal set and happened to hear your program. Reception was not good but she stuck to it and every Sunday she got it the best she could and enjoyed it so much. About three Sundays later she asked me to listen, but I would not. Then, knowing I loved music, she asked me please to listen to the piano and to hear the male quartet. I at last gave in and listened. The music was even better and prettier than she could tell me about. A few Sundays later I asked her if I could have one of the ear phones. She gave me one and she kept the other. It was difficult to hear, but I plugged my other ear and thus we both got the benefit of your wonderful program. About three months ago we got a radio and then Father, Mother and I all listened. I would like very much to be converted, so I am writing asking you to pray for me and also for my brother. Although we have both been raised in a good Christian home we have wandered away. But I should like to come back.

From northern California: My husband and I listen to the Old Fashioned Revival Hour every Sunday night and we certainly do enjoy it. Neither of us are saved, but listening to you certainly makes us want to walk with God. Won't you pray for us that we may enter into the fold. I could listen to you preach all night.

From the University of California: As I listen to your choir sing, "Jesus Saviour, Pilot Me," I write this letter, trying to find the Master through hazy darkness. My father was a minister for thirty-four years. I have strayed from the faith and I cannot seem to find my way back. Will you please pray for me.

"Just a sinner": I have committed every crime that God says, "Thou shalt not." Long, many years ago, when I was nine years old, I was baptized, but that didn't mean a thing. When I was eighteen or nineteen I was baptized again. Believe me, I fully intended to follow Christ then, but the devil got me sure. I committed murder—two of them—because I drifted so far away, but, thank God, I am awake now to really what I am, just a sinner, a terrible sinner.

From Texas: I listened to your sermon tonight on "the harvest is past and summer is ended, and we are not saved." When you pleaded with the listeners to search their hearts, I knew that I was not a Christian and I've known it for a good while. I feel that the coming of the Lord is near and

I want to be ready. But I know that I'm treading on dangerous ground and I feel that if my home as well as my soul is saved I must find the Lord very, very soon.

From Oregon: I hardly know how to write to you, but I am old and I don't know how to be saved. I know Jesus died for sinners on the cross, and I am a sinner and want to get saved. I am a lost soul. Will you please pray for me.

A dissatisfied college graduate: Tonight I heard your program for the first time and I am writing to ask you to pray for me. I am twenty-six years old and have two college degrees. I have never had any Christian instruction, nor have I ever been in a Christian home. It may seem strange to you but we have never had a Bible in our home. My parents do not believe in religion.

I have had such unrest for the past year—cannot see anything in this life. I finished college with honors and have a good position, but do not want to live unless I have something to live for, and will kill myself if this continues, as I am bored with this life. I just play bridge, and dance, and go with boys to these dumb parties, and I do not want to do that all the rest of my life, for these are such empty things. I never heard anything like you had on your Hour tonight, and it appealed to me. Perhaps there is something to live for after all. I do not know one person who would pray with me or who cares whether my soul is lost or not. These young people spend much time telling how they do not believe in God, yet I am not so sure there is not a God, and I should like to believe in Him. I long for real peace and joy, and I cannot just go on living this way. I shall be listening next Sunday evening, and will you please pray for me. (Note: The writer of this letter has since come out into a beautiful Christian experience and is serving God today.)

From a boy in his teens: I have been listening to your broadcast of the gospel for four or five Sunday nights now, and every time I hear it it makes my heart ache for the full know-so salvation. You know the saying is, "Just one step away from God is a million miles from home." That is just how close and yet how far away from Christ I am.

My folks are sinners, and it seems that I am the only one in the family who wants to have eternal life, and sometimes it seems hopeless for me to even try to pray for it. The folks have a big radio set, and they tuned in to your service just once. After that I got me a little crystal set so when I go upstairs I never sleep until your service is over. I can never tell you what it means to me. I would gladly send you some money to help, but I have no work.

Two lives saved: Wood you be interested to no that your program saved my life tonite, and not only my life but my husband; he had been drinking and got awful mad because he said we was getting old. And was not getting any place in the world and he said he was going to kill me and hiself. The he hurd the radio singing Never Give Up, and he got to listening, and he cried and kissed me and we promised wed listen every Sunday nite and never give up no more again. Love to you and Mrs. Fuller.

15

SOME CAN GIVE ONLY A LITTLE—OTHERS NOTHING

M ANY PEOPLE imagine that the Old Fashioned Revival Hour is made possible financially by the gifts of wealthy men. This is not the case. While there are occasionally fairly large gifts, the fact is that the program could not continue for a single week were it not for the sacrificial support of those who are able to give only very small amounts. The following letters are typical of many received each week from these humble and devoted supporters of the work. In times of special crisis, such as the summer of 1938, when several of these letters were written, even the poor have had great joy in finding special ways to "do without" for the sake of the gospel.

From Oregon: We want you to know how happy we are helping you to win souls for Christ. We thank God for this opportunity. One Sunday, several weeks ago, I tuned in for your program. I couldn't get it. If you only knew what a feeling came over me. I almost cried and I thought, "Oh, I didn't send in enough to help Mr. Fuller." I rushed out where my husband was choring and told him about it.

He said I must be mistaken. I came back and turned on the radio and there was your program. I don't know why I didn't get it the first time but maybe it was to make me realize how really precious your program is, so I'll send my little bit in more regularly. I want to send extra to help out this month that has *five* Sundays.

A recent convert in Michigan: Last Sunday I had a chance to preach to forty people, and they gave me a dollar collection. Then, last night, I heard you say that you could preach to twelve hundred people for one dollar, so I am sending my pay to you. Have been saved only eighteen months, so you can imagine how thin my sermon must have been; but several of the saints nodded their heads as I talked about the necessity for the new birth. I am no preacher, not even a layman, not even a hedgerow preacher. I could be described only as a bush-whacker. I whack the bushes, and if a bird flies out I present the truth and how God saves us. It has been a source of great pleasure to kneel with a man and see him born again. Do you think that prayer without money would help? I haven't been able to give you much money, but I have your name on my daily prayer list. . . . The two men in state prison can never hear you, but they are only recently saved and your messages in the Heart-to-Heart Talks will help their growth in Christ.

A love gift: I listen to your talks over the radio, every Sunday evening, and receive so much good from them. I am like the lady with the three dimes. I myself haven't much money but my two sons were drowned twenty-six years ago. I have kept this money ($1.25) that they had. They were young. One was thirteen and the other seventeen. I have never felt like parting with it, but think it will help spread the good work you are doing. God bless you. Hope you can continue on and on. I love the singing very much.

An amusing and interesting letter: I wondered what I could do without on Monday so that I could help the Old Fashioned Revival Hour. I thought I would get some dried beans and eat them and no meat on Monday. I never did like dried beans, but I knew that ten cents' worth would last for four Mondays, and it would take a dollar's worth of pork chops to last that long, so was I surprised when I went to eat the beans that they were the best tasting beans I ever ate. So I am sending you the dollar. If people that have plenty of this world's goods were in my place for a while and they couldn't hear a word when they went to church because they were deaf, they would give to help the Old Fashioned Revival Hour. May the Lord bless you all.

A Washington giver: When I heard your suggestion on the radio that we sacrifice something on Monday during the summer to help carry on the Old Fashioned Revival Hour I began wondering what we could sacrifice, and immediately the Lord seemed to speak to me so plainly, "Sacrifice your cream." So on Mondays I just fill up our cream pitcher with milk and rejoice that we can have a part in this small way in helping send out the good news of the gospel, and we pray that many folks may be saved.

Another fine suggestion: My father's birthday was this month. He passed away just a year ago, but rather than send flowers to put on his grave I am sending the dollar to you to use in your gospel work.

From an aged woman in Washington: I will enclose one dollar to help send the gospel to lost souls. I don't have much of this world's goods. I am over seventy years old, but I walked over five miles to the woods and picked one gallon of wild berries and sold them for one dollar. So I will send it for the radio, to spread the gospel. I told the Lord if He would give me strength I would do my part. He helps in every way.

Elderly folks in Michigan who had found Christ: My husband and I have listened to your sermons for over a year. They have meant so much to us. We have accepted Christ as our personal Saviour since listening to you.

We are old people and have very little to do with. Sometimes it is hard for us to make expenses, but we manage to live. We are willing to economize this week so as to be able to send a little to help keep up your wonderfully good work. I must hasten now and get this in the mail so you will get it this week.

From Tacoma, Washington: There is a history connected with two of the dollars that I am sending to help carry on your work. Years ago, my youngest brother gave me, at different times, silver dollars. I always kept them thinking I would buy something with which to remember him, for he went to be with the Lord in 1925. But I still have them. Well, the other week, it came to my mind that the best I could do with them was to send them to help give out the story of Christ over the air. I know nothing could have pleased my dear brother better than to know it was doing something for the Lord.

Evidently a sacrificial giver: I hope to send ten cents each Monday this summer. We live on a small farm and don't go to town often, as we have to go with a team. I hope the small amount that I am able to send will help a little.

The pennies are saved: It seems so hard to find something to do without when one always considers twice before getting anything, so I eat a little more breakfast and then I do without lunch. I am going to save all my pennies—that is, I am not going to spend the pennies I get for change but send them to you for spreading the gospel.

This little boy's bank helped: We had a little boy and had to give him up. He was our only child. He had a little box he called his bank that he kept his pennies in. We had wondered so much what to do with it and when we heard you read about others we decided we would send his to you. You can't know, unless you have had the experience, just how much one treasures these little things. I know if he knew we were sending his little bank to you for this cause he would be so delighted, for he always enjoyed giving pennies at Sunday school. We deeply regret not having taught him more about Jesus, but we did teach him that God was the creator of everybody and everything good. He went before he quite reached the age of nine.

I want to say a few words about ourselves. We were raised up in Christian homes in the South. We were baptized early in life and sincerely believed we were saved, as we didn't indulge in worldly things. When we had to give up our boy, about a year and a half ago, we knew we were not ready to go where he went. It seems so strange things have to happen that way to make one see. We began to read our Bibles with a desire to know and understand. How different it all is. I am afraid there are many others in the same way we were. They think they are saved when they are not. I hope people will heed your advice to read their Bibles. We live on an oil lease in a Mennonite settlement. We are sending our little boy's box just as it is. We don't feel like handling the money ourselves. I know you will understand.

Instead of a vacation trip: I surely enjoy your broadcasts Sunday after Sunday, and pray that you may stay on the air until Jesus comes. I am sending you twenty-five dollars which I could have used for a vacation trip. I was promised a trip by my father and mother, to visit my relatives whom I have not seen for two and a half years. There was a longing in my heart to be back there once again. I was planning on going and was preparing my things. The Sunday before I was to leave the question came to me, "Are you willing to give that to God for the spread of the gospel?" All sorts of different things came to my mind, the pleasures I would miss if I did not go, and the question of whether I would ever get a chance to go again. Praise God, He helped me through it all and that is why I am sending the twenty-five dollars, and trust the Lord will bless and multiply it. I am seventeen years old and for some time I have been wondering what I could sacrifice for the gospel.

Three dimes: I am in receipt of your very kind and helpful letter and literature, for which I thank you. I am enclosing thirty cents—three dimes turned black from lying ten years in a little bank left by my little, departed son. Somehow I have never wanted to part with these little dimes until now. I feel that, although a very small sum, it may help to spread the gospel message to hungry souls such as mine. I feel that, could my little boy speak, he would wish his little savings to be sent out on a mission for Christ. Oh, how I pray that the Old Fashioned Revival Hour will never have to discontinue because of lack of funds. I feel sure that our dear Lord will supply its needs. There are many of us here, in the T.B. sanatorium, who look forward to each Sunday evening when we join with many millions in this wonderful inspirational hour around our radio.

A lady in Portland, Oregon, writes a very touching letter: Years ago, when my son was a little boy, my mother sent these two dimes to him to buy something for his birthday. I could not decide what to buy and before I did decide God called my mother home. I could not bear to use the money and have kept them all these thirty-five years. Now I know what to do with them. I will send them to you to help buy station time—my mother's money and my boy's present. The boy, of course, is now a man grown. May God bless these two little dimes to His glory.

From Brooklyn, New York: When my little son, two

years old, went to be with Jesus in 1912, he had his little bank account. This I am now sending out to you to help just a little in bringing Christ as Saviour to the hearts who have never even once heard the gospel.

A Christmas suggestion for others to follow: I am cutting out gift wrapping paper, cards, seals, and soforth, on my Christmas packages in order to send this dollar to help on your program. We feast on the Heart-to-Heart Talks which come to us every two weeks.

From a Washington widow: I am a widow woman with three children. I haven't words to say how much we enjoy the Old Fashioned Revival Hour. I am hoping and praying that you may stay on the air. My mother sent me this dollar for a Christmas present and I have decided to send it to help carry the gospel.

A British Columbia pig and three dollars: The batteries of my radio set are gone and now I cannot listen to your words of comfort. But God has been so good to me that I know He will fix things for me so I will not be too downhearted. I could not help any, last month, but I traded some hay for a little pig and three dollars, so I am sending two dollars and pray that the good work will be carried on and the gospel spread over the land.

Two nickels: Upon listening to your program tonight for the first time, I heard you read a letter in which a little mother sent a small bank account which was left by her little child of two who had been called Home long ago. It touched me so deeply, as twenty-three years ago my little girl of the same age was called away. It seemed she was all I had and we were so poor. She had a little celery salt shaker with two nickels in it. When she would go to bed at night and even the few days that she was ill, she would shake it and smile when she heard it jingle. All these years I have treasured the memory of that baby smile. Will you please take these nickels and let them help send out the gospel. It may not mean very much, but oh, they are so dear to me. Yet I want them used for God. Thank you for the comfort of this wonderful and inspiring program.

One of the greatest joys to Mr. and Mrs. Fuller and their associates is that even the poorest of the poor hear the gospel. Many do not attend church services because they lack suitable clothing for a public gathering. Others have no means of transportation. Still others are kept away because they are embarrassed over not being able to contribute. To all such persons the Old Fashioned Revival Hour is a God-sent means of giving out the gospel.

I am just a poor colored man and I wash windows when I get the work. Our home is only a shack on a back alley and these cold winds do blow in pretty bad, but it's a happy home because my wife and I and our oldest girl are Christians. And, say, do we love to hear you preach and sing! Your songs come into our little shack just the same as they do to the fine houses where the rich folks live. My mother is eighty-eight years old and lives with us. She likes the old time songs you sing, and stomps her foot to keep time.

From New York City: Something told me to listen to a sermon last Sunday. I just happened to tune in and, to my surprise, I found just what I wanted and needed. In all my life I have never heard the Word of God spoken like this. I want to tell you it has changed me. I am a full fledged Christian now. Here are the words which helped me. "Though your sins be as scarlet they shall be as white as snow." Please pray for me. I am not able to send an offering but hope to later.

From the Dust Bowl: What can a fellow who can hardly sit up say! The family just sits around watching the clock on Sunday evenings for the time to tune in on the radio, for the song, "Jesus Saves." The tears flow when the music, the greeting, the sermon, and the sweet voice of Mrs. Fuller come in. We are hard hit down here in the dust bowl, so we can't even send postage for the Heart-to-Heart Talks, as much as we would like to yet. It snowed and possibly we shall be able to raise some wheat and barley again. A baby died here three days after birth because the mother had been starved. This was the doctor's verdict.

From San Francisco, a newsboy writes: I am a high school boy and glad to send a little which I have earned selling papers, to help carry on your blessed work of spreading the gospel. We listen to it regularly.

Real devotion to Christ: I know that lots of people are hungry for the Word of God, and I want to help as much as I can. My husband cuts my hair and I cut his hair, and we don't go to any pleasure places, so we can help a little bit more. We just love to hear the letters and it touches our hearts to hear of the sacrifices of others. I wondered how I could pinch out more on our expenses, and I thought of one way to save out a dollar for your broadcast, and that was to fix my old shoes that needed half soles. This usually costs over a dollar. But I went to the ten cent store and bought a pair of rubber soles and I put them on, myself, and here is my dollar along with the others. The rubber soles feel much better, too. I have received so many blessings as I have listened in to your messages, but I just couldn't keep it all to myself, so I had to send fourteen invitations to friends in Oakland, California, to listen in to the Old Fashioned Revival Hour and get an ear full and a heart full of the Bread of Life.

16

ARE YOUNG PEOPLE INTERESTED?

I F MR. FULLER were a "great preacher" according to the standards of many intellectuals he would probably have failed utterly to get his message into the hearts of the children and young people whose letters are given here.

The wonder of God's method of evangelism is that He "hath chosen the foolish things of the world to confound the wise; and . . . the weak things of the world to confound the things which are mighty; and base things of the world, and things which are despised, . . . and things which are not, to bring to nought things which are; that no flesh should glory in His presence."

Men preparing for the ministry are more and more prone to spend weary years of study to earn another coveted degree, many times losing their intimate touch with their Lord and the problems of humanity in the process of getting an education. In the case of Mr. Fuller, as in that of Dwight L. Moody, God chose to demonstrate the greatness of His power by taking a man from the business world, with little theological training, and making him one of the greatest soul winners of this generation.

Two little boys in Washington: I want to tell you of the joy I had the other evening. Three weeks ago I was called into a home to care for two little boys while their parents were in New York for the month of March. As I always listen to your program at home I just turned the radio on here. The first time they said, "That is a nice program." And then last Sunday we listened again. The oldest boy, ten years of age, said, "That is wonderful. Oh, I like it." He listened very intently until you were finished. Then he turned to me and said, "I believe it. Tell me, what shall I do now to be saved." So we went down to our knees before God and the boy was really saved.

A little girl writes: I am only nine years old. Last Sunday night while you were preaching I felt I needed Jesus. I went to my room, got down on my knees and asked Christ to forgive my sins. Mamma and Daddy say I have been a lot better girl since. When I think of confessing my sins a verse in the Bible comes to me. "If we confess our sins He is faithful and just to forgive us our sins and to cleanse us from all unrighteousness." I just love the Old Fashioned Revival Hour.

A letter from Canada: It is with a thankful and happy heart that I write to you this time. My youngest brother-in-law was converted on February 5, after listening to the Old Fashioned Revival Hour. He is just sixteen years old and we are so thankful that he has found Christ so young. Just as you were closing the hour and were speaking to the people outside of Christ, asking them to come, Kenneth slid off his seat to his knees and accepted Christ as his personal Saviour right there. When he got up he told his mother

AMERICA BACK TO GOD
GOOD FRIDAY SERVICES 1938
OLYMPIA - DETROIT
12000 PEOPLE ATTENDING

PHOTO-SPENCER A NYCHOFF

that he certainly had a heavy burden of sin before but Christ had taken it all away.

A fine letter from a boy in Iowa: I am a sophomore in High School. I have a paper route so make my own money. Each week my tithe is taken out first and it is from this fund that I am sending this small donation, hoping that it will be the means of bringing your message to some other high school boys who do not have the opportunity of attending Sunday school and church each week as I do.

From Indiana a high school senior writes of God's saving grace: I am the oldest of nine children and a senior in high school. I hardly ever get a chance to attend church services, but each Sunday night I try to get to listen to your service. Tonight I listened and never heard the way made so plain. It seemed that Mr. Fuller was preaching right at me. Now I know that the Lord saves me. I never felt His presence as I feel it tonight, and I felt that I must in some way testify as I can't go to church. So I am testifying by writing to you.

Another little girl writes as follows: I am a girl twelve years of age and have a sister five years old. Our mother has been in bed since August, 1936, with T.B. We cannot go to church very often as our mother is in bed and our only neighbors are two aged women. We tuned in tonight to get you. We have our radio in my mother's room and tonight she twisted the dial until she found you and then said in a happy way, "There they are." My sister and I went to the library table and got two Bibles, one for Mother and one for Daddy. Your program has been our only church service for a long time. God has been helping Mother to get well.

Here is a good letter from a lad who was recently converted: The thirty cents I am sending you would, more than likely, have been spent for ice cream and candy if I had not listened to your program tonight. When I heard how great the need is now, I thought this little bit might help. I was saved while listening to your program last November. My mother had been talking to me about Christ for some time and that night I believed.

I am a girl of seventeen. I keep house for my father in a little mill town of about three hundred population. My mother died when I was ten years old. Father and I are carrying on alone. It's hard when only seven people out of three hundred profess to believe Jesus. We live seventeen miles from town and have no car. You can't imagine what your Hour means to two lonely hearts. We have had family prayer ever since I can remember. I have always believed in God but when you preached on faith last night, I really became a child of God. I really prayed through and feel the Spirit of God.

This girl in Louisiana also found the Lord: Ever since I received your letter and booklets I have been deeply convicted. Sunday evening I got down upon my knees and asked God to forgive me of my sins. Thank God He did. Now I know Him and have joy in reading my Bible and listening to God's Word. Every time I feel down and out I get your letter and my Bible and read to make fresh in my mind my hope of another world to come. I haven't been going to Sunday school, but now I am going and this Sunday I am going to join the church. Mother and Dad said I could not join until I was converted. I intend to tell others of God's salvation and that Jesus saves. When I get my Bible down to read my sisters and brothers come and sit at my feet for me to teach them. There is no church within about eight miles of here. Some never hear God's Word.

From a farm girl in Alabama: We listen almost every Sunday night to the Old Time Revival Hour. It has been a blessing to us all, especially me. I was saved last night, while your service was going on. A prayer that you prayed touched my heart. I was already under conviction but I tried to fight it back. Praise God, I couldn't and I am now a child of God.

My family is a sinful one. They don't know God. Please help me pray for them. I am a girl of fourteen years of age and hope to keep the old time salvation in my heart.

From a college girl: I am a college girl, so of course I am kept very busy with my class work but every Sunday evening I stop working and take time to listen to your program, which I enjoy so much. Your songs are most beautiful and Mr. Fuller has answered so many questions in my mind through his sermons. I am a senior, this year, and I am so glad we have been given the privilege of having radios in our rooms in the dormitory so that I and many others may hear your program. I listened to Rev. Fuller's message on "Prayer" several weeks ago and I do pray very humbly and beg God to forgive me and help me to face my trials and solve my problems.

A C.C.C. boy: My happiest moments are when I read your Heart-to-Heart Talks and my Testament out in the woods with the birds and everything that is God's around and about me and think how nice Heaven is. I am sending this to you to help spread the gospel. I am just a C.C.C. boy from Ohio.

Another in Oregon: A C.C.C. boy came to our house looking for a small radio to buy. We asked if he ever listened to *your* program. His face lighted up like the morning sun and he said, "That's why I want a radio." He had heard you and wanted to have others at the camp hear you, too.

One lady writes that her three boys, 12, 13 and 16 years old, always rush in and ask if they are in time to hear Mrs. Fuller read the letters. They just hurry through the chores to get to hear the whole program.

And here is a letter from a mother: For some time my thirteen year old son has listened with me to your Sunday night program. One night I was away and he tuned in and told me of it later, although it comes at the same hour as a national program which all the boys seem to love. A couple of weeks ago he said, "Mother, the first money I get for selling a chicken I am going to send to the Fullers." In a few days he sold a chicken, and here is the money. Pray that my boy may give his heart to Christ and that he may grow up to love and serve Him. He has no one but me to help him.

From a children's home in Alaska: Every Sunday evening, as the strains of "Jesus Saves" come floating through our radio, up the steps into the living room comes a band of eager children all ready to listen to the program. Their ages range from seventeen to three years. There are many nationalities represented. While giving the morning lesson on Monday this week, on Proverbs 3:9, I asked the children if they had any tithing they wanted to give, to honor the Lord. Up went several hands. I brought a plate and then they began to bring pennies, nickels, and dimes. Then some of the older ones had a larger amount of money. We then figured out that if every child in America would give a penny there would be sufficient money to carry on this great gospel broadcast. We herewith send this offering of twenty dollars, the tithe of the money which they were to spend in town on the 4th of July. Though it was a sacrifice it was a blessing to them to give and we are sure that God will bless it as we place it in your hands to use for sending out this glad and glorious message of salvation.

I am a matron in an orphanage. My girls and myself can hardly wait until Sunday night comes so we may hear your program. My girls are from nine to twelve and they are fine, sweet girls, and your talks are so helpful to them.

I am eighteen years of age and, this day, I prayed and asked God to accept me. I want to live a Christian life.

Yes, I have accepted Him as my Saviour and I want to learn more of Him so I am going to continue to listen to your broadcast.

I am a boy thirteen years old and I listen to your program every Sunday. Tonight I have given my heart to God and my sins have been washed away in the blood of Christ. Pray for me, that I may be faithful. I feel that I should help in your great work for the Master. I have earned a dollar and am sending it to you as I love to hear the Word of God.

From Massachusetts: I listened to your program for the second time, last night. I am a boy of sixteen who hadn't thought much of this wonderful subject of following the Lord. I am trying to live a life that will bring a rich reward when I am called Home. Your program is like a shining light in this world of darkness. While listening, last evening, I resolved that from then on I would ask the Lord to give me the strength to live up to His pattern of life. I know now that it gives you a wonderful feeling to get down on your knees and in solitude ask God to wipe the slate clean and allow you to start afresh in an effort to please Him and to pray to Him as a real friend and Saviour.

I just received my money on a hog I sent to market and I am giving a tenth for the Lord. Am sending it to be used in your work. I am a red-headed thirteen year old boy who loves his Lord dearly.

From Oregon (More of this is needed): On Sunday, October 15th, we were all around the radio listening to your program when suddenly one of our granddaughters began to weep and cry out to God for forgiveness. Then one by one three more of them came to the Lord that evening and were gloriously saved. They've been very different girls since then. I am so thankful.

From northern California: I am a boy sixteen years old and I give a tithe of what I earn to the Lord, so I thought

I would send you this offering, as I surely enjoy your radio broadcasts. Am thankful to say I am born again and I pray for your broadcast that it may be able to continue.

From a high school Junior in Chicago: I have listened to the Old Fashioned Revival Hour for several months now and I don't see how I could have been as I was before. I really decided to be a Christian and bear the cross. Oh, I can't express how happy and how good I feel now, and how different. I am fifteen and in my third year of high school. I tried out for the basketball team last fall. I had never played it much before and I saw many boys better than me quit and give up trying. But I thought to myself that I would have faith because God would not want me to be a quitter and give up. I tried hard and I made the team. I am sending you a little money to help keep you on the radio because you have shown me the right way. You probably know that there are some who swear and say filthy things but although I have been around I never do anything like swearing, drinking or smoking. I am going to try to make something out of myself for Christ's sake. I get your Heart-to-Heart Talks and I like them swell, especially the poems. I live in Chicago, but wherever I go God is with me.

From Massachusetts: In your sermon tonight when you said, "Behold the Lamb of God," your message was not only for aged people. I am an eighteen year old girl and I can honestly say that nothing satisfies the heart but Christ. I wonder if other young people, tonight, can't join in with me and say "Amen" to that. I tried the world and I thought "There's time enough later to think about Christ. He'll wait. That stuff is for those who are old and ready to die." But when I got a glimpse of the beauty of Christ I was drawn to Him and, tonight, I rejoice that I have a life of youth to give to Him for His service. I am taking training expecting that

I may tell the blessed Chinese souls of this wonderful Lamb of God.

A seven year old: I was saved by hearing you preach over the radio and I will always remember when I was saved, in 1938. I am seven years old now. I want you to pray for me and my mother, and here is some money I earned.

I am a young man who loves your program. Every Sunday night I hurry with my milking and other chores to get through in time for the very first part of the song, "Jesus Saves," and I think, as I work fast, of the other boys on the farms who are hurrying to listen, too. I wish I could know some of them, for I would like to have a Christian friend. None of my family cares to listen but my mother and me. We let the others have the radio all day so we can listen to "Our Hour," and your quartet music is the sweetest music we have ever heard. We live way out in the country. We have learned so much more about God's Word. You make it so plain, Mr. Fuller, and now we know, mother and I, that though things are so hard, yet God is directing our path and will help us.

From unchurched young people in Montana: Almost every Sunday for two winters we've been listening to your sermons. I think they are wonderful and I wish I could have all your sermons in a book so I could read them over and over. I am just a young girl starting out in life and you are just wonderful for young people to listen to. I have from eight to eleven young people (16 to 22) in my home to listen to you each Sunday night and four of them have found the Lord through you, one of them was my brother. He is nineteen and I am eighteen.

We are ninety miles from our closest town and in this community we haven't a religious gathering of any kind. In all our life we haven't attended a Sunday school. We are thirty miles from where they have church and that is in a school house. I don't know why there aren't more ministers like you. I think in a little while we that listen to you each Sunday will be able to send a little. I would love to have your Heart-to-Heart Talks . . . I know of twenty-one families that listen to you in this county and of three families in South Dakota, though they have not sent their names in.

From a boy in jail: I am well pleased with your Talks. My Grandma goes to church every Sunday night and brings me something to read. For I am in jail and might go to prison for about fifteen years. I am only eighteen years old. Will you please send me something you think will help me. Some books of the Bible or some more written statements (Talks) I am pleased with your radio programs.

17

IN SUCH STRANGE PLACES TO HEAR THE GOSPEL

God makes even the wrath of man to praise Him. How often it happens that in the most ungodly places, where the radio is used entirely for jazz and swing music, the failure to tune out the Old Fashioned Revival Hour when the time for a change in program comes results in the gospel gaining an entrance where no person could go with the Word of Life. Often, even here, the message brings conviction as it falls on good ground.

A Salvation Army lassie writes from the North: Two of us corps cadets have taken to passing out tracts in the bars. We thought you might be interested in one of our experiences. While my friend was going around handing out her tracts, I saw a small radio in the corner of the bar room. It was just time for you to come on the air, so I walked over to the radio which was playing jazz full blast and I turned back the dial until I heard the familiar strains of "Jesus Saves." I expected the owner to yell at me to "turn that off," but he didn't and neither did the men. They just sat and listened.

Whenever I go in there now, the men say, "Here comes Mr. Fuller's little missionary." They really seem to enjoy it, and I hope it will win their hearts, for they surely need it.

Dear Mr. Fuller: We live out in the country, too, and don't get to church every Sunday, but we always listen to your program and thank the Lord for it. The singing is wonderful, and what I like about Brother Fuller's messages is that he uses so much of God's Word. I have intended to write you many times but something always hinders, but tonight I am going to do what the other party that you read about did: I am going to milk in the moonlight so that I can hear you. Please send me ten or twelve radio logs as all my people are unsaved, living in Canada and California. I want them to listen to your broadcast and I believe that God will save them.

Another strange place: I listen regularly to the Old Fashioned Revival Hour when I am at home. Recently when I was away from home in a northern city I wondered where I might hear this program, as I walked along the street and the time drew near to listen. I passed by a beer parlor and, to my surprise, in there I heard your program going on full blast. I went in, sat down, ordered a bottle of soda water and listened through. It was a strange place for me to be and a stranger place for me to listen to your program but, thank God, it was going out there and was being listened to.

The cows enjoy listening, too: Last Sunday, we were on a drive with some friends and were a little late getting home to turn on the radio. We stopped to look at a pond close to a farm house and, lo and behold, the Idaho farmer had a radio in the cow barn and the Old Fashioned Revival Hour was being broadcast to everyone in general. This idea of radios in cow barns seems to be catching!

From a young man on one of the battleships in San Pedro Harbor, in California: You don't know what your program means to the men of the fleet. Wherever we go we are able to receive your program. Some of us talk to folks in various ports about the Old Fashioned Revival Hour and we find many listeners everywhere. We are indeed happy that we listen in, whether we are ploughing through the high seas or whether we are in port. Please pray for us and we will pray for you. (Signed, "A Christian sailor")

On a train: As I was traveling on the train from Denver to Pennsylvania to visit my aged mother for Christmas the radio was turned on and I was so glad that so many had a chance to listen to the Old Fashioned Revival Hour, for that is the program that was tuned in for us.

Gas station men like to listen, too: I don't know what we would do if you were off the air on Sundays, for we have a gas station and we have to stay open. We have an eleven-tube radio and we put it in the window and it can be heard a long ways off. Many cars stop long enough, while they get gas, to hear a good part of the preaching and we call everybody's attention to the service, and we sing along with you. People stop and listen. This last Sunday night, one man came in and heard the quartet singing and he said, "Who is that? I never heard them before," and he went right out and turned it on in his car.

Do chickens like the music, too? For some time I have not been able to listen, as I have had to pack eggs Sunday nights for early Monday morning delivery, but now we have an old radio set up in the egg house, and the last two Sundays we have been able to listen again. How I have enjoyed it. Have received many blessings in the past through your broadcast and through the Heart-to-Heart Talks.

Imagine hearing the gospel in a saloon! While I am writing, I want to tell you about an incident that happened to a cousin of mine in Denver. He was there on a visit and not familiar with the city. One Sunday he was looking for a drug store and, thinking he had found one where he might be able to hear the program, entered to discover that it was a liquor store. But the thing that held him in his tracks, amazed, was a radio turned on and a group of men gathered round listening so earnestly to the program. It was yours.

From the belfry of a church: Last Sunday evening we were surprised and very glad to hear your program being broadcast through a loud speaker in the belfry of a small church at Big Harbor. It was loud and plain enough to be heard all through the town.

A young man in the South spreads the Good News: I am a saved young man and try to give out the gospel. I have a public address system, so I set my microphone in front of the radio last Sunday night, and ran the cord outside to my car. I broadcast your gospel service out on the street so that people a mile around could hear it. It sure sounded wonderful. The whole neighborhood heard the gospel, that night. So I thought I would help in that way in doing my share each Sunday night to see that you go on the air around here, so the unsaved may hear the gospel. They gathered around last Sunday in crowds to listen.

From a hotel room in Chicago: I am a young man, twenty-five years of age, a commercial traveler by occupation covering a territory from coast to coast in Canada. For some time I have been held by some supernatural power to my room on Sunday evenings and drawn to listen to your broadcast. Why I do not know because church has never held any place in my life. I feel you are so sincere in your talks. I am very seldom alone during your broadcast, as I always ask some of my traveling associates to join me. After the address tonight my friend turned to me and asked if I would pray for him before I retired. This I feel unworthy to do, so I am writing on his behalf and also for myself to ask you and your wife to breathe a prayer for us both to Him who knows our helpless state. We both realize that we are on the outside of the ark of which you spoke. I hope that through listening to your future broadcasts my heart shall find rest. Next Sunday night I shall be listening to you from Saskatchewan. Thanking you for your excellent program, I remain—"A heavy hearted young man."

Dear Mr. Fuller: I listen to your program every Sunday and like it fine. Last Sunday I had an hour or so before you would be on the air, so I went into a gambling joint to lose or win a little (I lost). Well, anyway, I got so busy watching the numbers I forgot about 7:30, when all of a sudden (in the gambling joint) the program changed and your program started. Well, I didn't play any more. I got in my car, tuned in to you and went home.

Just wanted you to know that, when you came on the air, just lots of players in this gambling place quit playing, too. When you get away from the Lord you go down hill, don't you? I hope I come back up hill before it is too late. I am eight dollars behind now, so will send the other three dollars soon. But it won't be gambling money.

Even on a bicycle vacation they are still members of the audience: My husband and I do so enjoy the Old Fashioned Revival Hour. It means so much to us that we do not want to miss a single program. Although long anticipating our vacation we were also worried about missing your program while away from the city. Our vacation plan is to travel through New England and part of Canada on our bicycles. And now the problem of hearing your program has been solved as we have a portable radio on one of the bikes. It was a wonderful thrill recently to hear the Hour while on a week end trip. When the time arrived, we stopped and turned in to a near-by grove and listened to your wonderful music. In the darkness it carried up through the trees. Brother Fuller's voice was so much in earnest and so sincere that I wonder how any reasonable person could let such a wonderful salvation pass them by. We will be starting on our trip very soon and plan to listen every Sunday wherever we may be.

A portion of the audience was in an Arkansas restaurant: We were sitting in a restaurant, last Sunday night, and the radio was on. The old gospel hymns of the Revival Hour were being sung. They arrested my attention. Our party became so interested that we stayed to hear the entire program. There was quite a congregation listening there in the restaurant. We finally passed a hat and are sending the offering to help pay for station time for the Old Fashioned Revival Hour.

From New Jersey: Your radio broadcast is the brightest spot in our family life. I am a traveling man, visiting every large city in the United States. This keeps me away from home, but every Sunday night there is a radio service where my family and I can worship together although far apart, thanks to your broadcast.

18

IN THE VALLEY OF THE SHADOW

B Y THE law of averages several thousand persons listen
to the Old Fashioned Revival Hour each Sunday
night who will never live to hear another gospel message.
It is a solemn thought. The reaction of most of these to
the message can never be known, but occasionally a letter
tells the story.

From Washington State: My dear husband loved your
program so much and never missed hearing it. He went
Home one Sunday evening with a smile on his face ten minutes after your broadcast closed. The enclosed money was
in his pocketbook and I am sure that he would like to send
it to you to help carry on your wonderful work.

A Long Island woman writes: A dear sister was saved, one
Sunday night, after your service, and two weeks later the
Lord called her Home to be with Himself. We are so
thankful that she heard the way of salvation and accepted
Christ as her Saviour.

Dear Mr. Fuller: How thankful I am you always give the
call for people to accept the Saviour, especially after hearing

of two people perishing in a burning house who were listeners to your program. The son, a man of fifty years, lived with the parents. The mother was nearly blind and the father very hard of hearing. The son had gone to the post office for the mail, that evening, and returning home about nine o'clock found the house on fire. He rescued his mother and returned for his father, but they were overcome and both perished in the burning building. I don't know whether they were saved or not, but in speaking to my aunt, who knew them well, about their souls she said, "They told me the last time I saw them that they listened to Mr. Fuller." I am so thankful that they had so many times heard the message and the way of salvation made plain. Am always so pleased to have you urge people to accept Christ.

Too weak to talk: The first time we heard your fine program was last fall as we were driving along the highway, and since then we have missed very few Sundays. Last Sunday, we went over to see my aged grandparents. He is eighty-four and Grandma is eighty. Grandpa can hardly move a finger and is so weak he cannot talk, but when he hears the familiar strains of "Jesus Saves" he moves his finger a little, which means that he wants us to turn the radio louder. We asked if he could hear and, with a little smile, he moved his head. Grandma tells everyone that comes to their house to be sure to listen to the Old Fashioned Revival. It's the best old fashioned preaching and singing she ever heard. The grand part of it is that it's still up-to-date.

The following clipping is from a newspaper: Mr. V. was in good health, apparently, earlier in the day and attended church services. After eating the evening meal, Mr. and Mrs. V. returned to their living room and were listening to the Charles Fuller radio program coming from California. A group of singers were singing, "When We All Get to

Heaven," and Mrs. V. remarked, "That will be a wonderful time, Daddy, when we all get to Heaven, won't it?"

He replied, "Yes." Instantly, Mrs. V. noticed his head fall to the back of the chair. "What's the matter, Daddy," she queried, and when Mr. V. failed to reply she went to the front porch and called for help. A physician was summoned but they found Mr. V. dead when they arrived.

My dear husband died in March. About two weeks before he went Home we were listening to your program. I had been praying for him for a long time. He was sitting by the fire when you gave the invitation. I went and put my hand on his shoulder and said, "Husband, when are you going to come back to your boyhood faith in God."

He looked up and said, with a sweet smile, "I am a Christian now." Words cannot express my deep joy and I thank you for helping him back to God.

From another bereaved family: Last evening we addressed a note to you with a small contribution in memory of my father whom we laid away on March 18th. He listened with us to your program on March 12th. In eagerly awaiting your broadcast, last evening, we could not know beforehand that you would bring words of comfort to those who were bereaved or that your musicians would sing so beautifully, seemingly just for us. The thought that the same message doubtless reached thousands of others whose hearts were grieved and who needed cheer or release from the burden of sin makes us wish from the bottom of our hearts that we were better able to support this God-given ministry.

Her last song on earth: On March 5, my dear mother was sitting by the radio listening to your program which came in so clearly. When you were singing, "What a Friend We Have in Jesus," she sang with them in a clear, strong voice, though ninety-six years of age. It will always be the most precious memory to me for it was her last song on earth. Before another Sunday evening she was too ill to sing and she went to her heavenly home on March 13.

Our dear mother went to be with the Lord in February. She listened regularly and greatly enjoyed every part of your service. Her last service was the one when you asked everyone to sing, "What a Friend." When you said, "Come on, Grandma, and sing," she sang with you for the last time.

A lady who is very ill writes a letter from a hospital bed: Those around my bed were listening to your program. When Mr. Fuller quoted the words, "Come unto me all ye that are weary and heavy laden and I will give you rest," the lady in the next bed put up her hand and said, "Lord, take me as I am." The nurse said, "How sweet you look. You have a smile that this old world cannot give." She may never see you here, Mr. Fuller, but some day you will know each other over there.

This husband found the Lord just in time: Just a few lines to give you a bouquet while you are living. I just can't wait until Sunday night to hear, "Jesus Saves," coming over the air from California. All the more so now because my dear husband was called Home to be with the Lord one night on his way home from work. He was a dear man, the best husband and father that could be. One thing I am so grateful about is that, about three Sunday nights before he died, he had been listening to your program. I came in the front room after putting the children to bed and he was down on his knees crying and asking God to forgive him and make him a better man. We both had backslidden. So I have that great comfort in knowing that he is at Home with the Lord and I have come back to Him, too. Do you wonder that we love the Old Fashioned Revival Hour?

Two hours later he passed away: Enclosed you will find

two dollars to help with your work. This morning my husband asked me to send this to you. Two hours later he passed away with heart failure. He did so love to hear you preach and to hear the songs, for he was a good Christian. It is so hard to think that he is gone, but I know that I will see him again—blessed hope.

From Oregon: I have an aunt who is now Home in glory, for it was through your service, on December 18, that Christ spoke to her. The following day she was taken sick with pneumonia. It proved her death bed, one week later. Your earnest pleading to accept Christ as a personal Saviour was heeded by her and she bore fruit that week before going Home by giving a ringing testimony for her Lord.

He is not afraid to die now: My husband has been helped so much by listening to your sermons. He says he is not afraid to die now and be with God. He is sending you one dollar in appreciation of your work. He has been bedfast for nearly a month now and is very weak. He is suffering so much—cancer is so very painful. I am sending my little bit, also.

A dying boy's testimony: I stood, this afternoon, by the bedside of a young man about twenty-three years of age. His earthly life was drawing very rapidly to a close. He could only speak with great difficulty. But he spoke some of the sweetest words I have ever heard. He said, "This wasted body of mine (and truly it was wasted, for it was in a T. B. cabin in a hospital) will return to the dust from which it came and my spirit will return unto God who gave it. But, oh, I am so glad I heard the good news of salvation before it was too late."

Last Easter Sunday, he told me, he had been listening to the Old Fashioned Revival Hour. Brother Fuller brought a message the previous Sunday evening which had touched his heart. He said, "All week it has been with me and there has been a great fight going on in my heart. At two o'clock this morning I awoke and gave my heart to God. I opened my heart's door and let Him come in. Now I have joy and peace. I will never get off this bed, but I want to do something for my Saviour who did so much for me."

Through the leading of the Holy Spirit he started to write and witness to shut-ins like himself. Every Sunday evening he has been listening to the Old Fashioned Revival Hour, but he can't listen tonight, Brother Fuller. I believe before morning he will hear sweeter music than mortal ear has ever heard. As long as I live those words he spoke this afternoon will ring in my ears.

Convicted that he had never been saved: I want to tell you how much your programs are helping us. My husband has been a professing Christian for years. He was taken sick with tuberculosis and has been sick for some time. Sunday night, he was listening to your program and when the chorus sang, "Beulah Land," he began to cry and was convicted that he had never really been saved. He asked us to pray for him and he was gloriously saved. He now says he is ready for whatever comes. He welcomes God's will. Please pray for him as he is going to the hospital.

Saved before it was too late: This Sunday evening hour is all too short. I want to tell you of a young couple who listened in and accepted Christ as a result of listening to your message. Soon after that the little bride was taken Home to be with the Lord. We are so glad that she was saved before it was too late.

She listened and then fell asleep: Our mother listened regularly to your broadcast for the last nine months of her life. She greatly enjoyed the music and messages and received much help and blessing therefrom. She also enjoyed the Heart-to-Heart Talks. She was confined to her bed for over two years. On July 16, she went to be with her Lord. On the evening of her departure the radio was tuned in to your program and, although Mother was very low, she recognized the music. About an hour later she quietly went to Heaven and faith became a reality.

19

GOD'S SHUT-INS

Before radio came, shut-ins were doomed to exclusion from church services. Now they can listen to messages which are food for the soul, join in the singing of familiar gospel songs, and have a sense of nearness to others in the great listening audience. The following letters tell a few of the many stories that might be told of those in such circumstances who have been immeasurably helped by Mr. Fuller's great radio ministry.

From Bronx, New York: My mother is a semi-invalid and unable to leave the house to go to church. She just waits for the Old Fashioned Revival Hour on Sunday night. You will never know just how much it means to her. I could never repay you for the untold pleasure and satisfaction you have brought to her.

I think it is only fair that you should know what a change there has been in my life since listening to your broadcast. I have always been what is termed "a good Christian," but I fear it was only skin deep. I had never really examined myself to find out just what kind of Christian I really was. After your broadcast I tried a little introspection. The findings were so awful I decided then and there to make it right with God. You have no idea of the difference in my life. The craving for worldly things has passed and I never thought it could. I hope it will be as much satisfaction to you as it is to me to know that it was your broadcast that clinched the proposition forever. I thank Him with my whole heart for all that He is to me.

From a sanatorium in Chicago: Quite a number of us T. B. patients listen in on your Sunday broadcasts. It pleases us so much to hear the Word of God given. We are Christians and it is the only way we can get to church. We feel that we are sitting right on the front row of your service, though we are bed-fast and so far away.

From a deaf listener in Austin, Texas: You do not know how I feel, humbly I say this, because you who hear with good ears could not understand. This evening, while sitting here alone in my room, I placed my little radio by my side and turning it on lay my hearing aid against it with only a faint hope that I might hear some sweet church music. I cannot describe to you my excitement when, over the radio, I heard a voice, clear as if speaking right by my side, then a song. And when I heard the voice say, "This is Los Angeles, California," I sat almost holding my breath, as I thought, "Is it possible, as deaf as I am that I am listening to a voice from Los Angeles, California?" My soul was tense with rapture as I sat listening for an hour to the songs and message for which my heart is so hungry. I never hear a sermon in the church. Oh, if only my boy in Los Angeles knew that the little radio he gave me was bringing his mother such pleasure, and if he were only listening to this message, too, and deciding for his mother's God tonight.

From an Indian patient in a New Mexico sanatorium: I

want you to know that I never fail to listen to the Old Fashioned Revival Hour. It has brought me to know our Lord Jesus. I am very thankful that I am sick and here in the sanatorium, for here I have given myself away to Him and have accepted Him as my personal Saviour. If I didn't get sick I might never have known Him. We are helping to win our fellow patients here by telling them of the precious Word of God, in English and Indian. I don't know if you ever hear from Indian boys and girls, but we love to listen to your program.

From a veteran's hospital: Your voice is now coming into my ear while the choir is singing, "God Will Take Care of You." I listen to you regular over my little table radio. I am a colored soldier. I have a lovely wife and sister whom I tell about your wonderful sermons. I don't get a pension from the government or the city for whom I worked ten years before Nov. 2, 1930, when I got my back broken. I am paralyzed and bedridden but I want to give God something, my heart included. This little sum is all I can afford, but it is from my heart to God.

From an aged Kansan listener: I live at the Rebecca Oddfellows' Home. I am eighty-two years old. We have one hundred and twenty old people here. We gather in a circle to listen to your gospel singers and your good sermon.

Lifted above the shadows: Words cannot express what the Old Fashioned Revival Hour meant to me tonight. The precious songs and message certainly lifted me above the shadows. I am one of several girls here in this hospital for tuberculosis. We listen in every Sunday night. The thought came to me that this precious gospel and the rich old hymns are not only for time but for eternity.

A shut-in in Iowa: "Be still and out of the stillness God will come to you." Friends, that is what my invalid mother and I experience every Sunday evening while we are tuned in on the Revival Hour. My mother is eighty-one. It will soon be four years since she has been able to attend church services. What a beautiful picture she makes sitting in her wheel chair transported in her enjoyment and keenly alert to every word which is being said. She repeatedly remarks, "To think it is coming sixteen hundred miles and still is so clear." What seems most remarkable to me is how the vibrancy and enthusiasm with which your voices are surcharged still retain cheer, virility and overtone of genuine, sympathetic love while they are travelling on the air waves.

From another sanatorium: My oldest daughter and I used to live together and got so much good out of your Revival Hour until the Lord called her home. Shortly after that I was taken sick and had to come to the sanatorium. I have no radio of my own and haven't been able to listen to you until two months ago when I was transferred to this ward. The girl in the bed next to me is also a good friend of the Old Fashioned Revival Hour. She lets me hook my ear phones up with her radio every Sunday night and we just have a grand time listening together.

From a lonely nurse in New York City: I was ready to turn off the radio last Sunday night, after listening to a local church service, when your hymn came over immediately afterward. As I listened my heart rejoiced that something so beautiful could be brought into my room, because earlier in the day I shed bitter tears of loneliness and homesickness, as I am away from friends and home. Being a nurse I can occupy my mind while on duty, but when off I find it trying alone in a large city like this.

Can you imagine what the program means to this shut-in from British Columbia? I enjoy your lovely services every Sunday night. It is the only real gospel meeting that I have heard since I was a child. I have been in bed, this time, for over seven years, so you can understand what I felt like when a dear old lady brought me a radio a year ago and I heard your service. It made me feel that there was someone still in this world who was wanting to let light in to some who are prisoners in sick rooms. It is just wonderful to have your splendid gospel message and the beautiful singing come to me here so far away.

Six years in a sanatorium in Pontiac, Michigan: May another tubercular patient add a word of praise and thanksgiving to God for your Old Fashioned Revival Hour. I know I speak for many here in our sanatorium as well as for the sick all over the land, when I tell you that your program, so free from all formality and strain, has its own special place in our hearts. We go to sleep immediately after listening in, and with lighter hearts for having heard the old, old story in a sweeter and simpler way. I am going into my sixth year here and only the Christ who met me here knows the song of praise that is in my heart tonight because He has dealt with me in this chosen way. I know that God has given me many special blessings which those who have not been laid aside miss. I am young, not quite twenty yet, and from the bottom of my heart I want to tell the world that Jesus satisfies all that a young person needs or wants, and I know that every other girl and boy who knows the Christ whom I know will say, "Amen." It is not just the whim of a sick girl.

A touching letter from Illinois: I enjoy your sermons so much, as I am an old man and a cripple. I have only one leg and this is partly paralyzed, so you can see I cannot get out to worship. I am the youngest grandson of a pioneer preacher and I have his old Bible which I prize very much. I am a poor man and cannot work. I have to get along on $14 a month caring for four, so you know how hard it is to manage. My wife and I try to sing with the choir those dear songs of long ago, and I sure do love to hear the Word proclaimed. Pray with us for our boy that he will forsake drinking and turn to God.

Heart-to-Heart Talks help the sick also: When Mr. Fuller comes to Boston next May I will meet him face to face and shake hands with him if I have to crawl there on my hands and knees. Words cannot express the joy and comfort that the Heart-to-Heart Talks bring to us. I use them in our church ladies' aid work and make them do double service by sending them to a sanatorium where they are passed from bed to bed, and many souls are being blessed by reading them.

From Colorado: I am a shut-in. I have had arthritis for many years and can't get out to church. I live with my widowed mother. My father passed away some thirteen months ago. I had two dollars given me for my birthday and I want you to have one of them to help carry on this great work which means so much to shut-ins.

In a home for the aged in Washington, D. C.: You have, in this home, a great congregation listening to your blessed services Sunday nights. The oldest one is ninety-eight years old. In a home of this nature your program is like a star lighted in the western sky. We all enjoy it more than we can tell, and thank you for it. We all send out notices of the Old Fashioned Revival Hour to our friends and daily uphold you in our prayers.

From a state hospital for tuberculosis in Oregon: I was feeling a little blue and lonesome for my children tonight when I tuned in on your program. When I heard the old hymns it reminded me of how much I have to be thankful for. There is nothing like gospel songs and the Word of God to comfort a lonely heart. Although I am so much better I cannot go home because my husband does not have steady work and even when I do go the doctor says I should not have any of the children at home with me. But God is good and He knows best, so I have no right to be down-hearted.

A terrible sufferer from arthritis: The Old Fashioned Revival Hour is the brightest hour in the whole week for me, also for my father who is eighty-nine years old and who lives with me. Nearly all my life, until a year ago, my Sundays were busy with three church services, and you can understand how void that day had become without any services. Truly God sent this program to me and to other shut-ins as well as to the unsaved.

From a T. B. sanatorium: I was stricken with tuberculosis last spring, so am in a sanatorium, but I am happy that I am still privileged to hear your broadcasts. The other day a vote was taken as to what night we preferred to have the radio on, as we are allowed only one evening a week. And I thank God that the majority voted for Sunday night and your program.

From another sanatorium: Many of the six hundred patients in this sanatorium listen to this Hour and love it.

From Yakima, Washington: We, the women of the county infirmary, want to tell you how much we enjoy your programs. We only wish we could help you with your broadcast. We all get near the radio in the sun room on Sunday nights where we can hear every word and the songs we like so very much. Indeed, we go back in our memories to the days when we were younger and used to stand in the choir and help sing many of the songs. How your music thrills us and helps us to think of things much brighter than earth, where we do not want to stay always. You make your messages so plain, how could anyone but understand them. We also like to hear the letters Mrs. Fuller reads over the air. We will be listening for you every Sunday evening.

GOD'S SHUT-INS

We gather in the sun room—some on crutches, some in wheel chairs, and we have our room just full to hear the gospel preached to hungry hearts. We all go to bed happy because we have the radio—a gift from an unknown friend to the women of this infirmary.

20

DEFEATED LIVES TRANSFORMED

M ANY ARE the stories of defeat and desperation from those who are suffering mentally and physically because of sin. Some of the most touching of these are from prison cells.

This letter is headed "On the Road"
Mrs. Charles E. Fuller, Dear sincere voice: I had to kill a man. Is there any redemption for a killer? Will be in another state by Sunday night, but will hear your voice in my car radio. (It was signed by a woman.)

From a redeemed drunkard: I just heard your message on the Good Shepherd. God bless you for the peace which has come in—the change in heart—the change in my whole life. Oh, what a tussle this has been as I have been driven away from my family while I had it out with myself and God. About two weeks ago I wrote you a very shaky and incoherent letter telling you I had just accepted Christ. I wouldn't exchange the last two weeks for all the rest of my twenty-eight years of lousy living. Like the man who had lain infirm for thirty-eight years, my body is also infirm from the drink habit. I don't know whether you realize it or not, but a man's habits can make him just as infirm as a physical accident. Maybe you don't know much about hobo jungles, but they are full of men who have no one to carry them into the pool, like that man in the Bible. A man never knows how deep in the mire of sin and drunkness he is until, all of a sudden, he tries to turn back. And it seems the old appetite is twice as strong as ever. Like the three blind men you told about, when you see you know you can see. I *know* I am saved, but I do so need your prayers. I am sending a quarter to help your work. This is all I have because I am on the absolute bottom, but I have granite underneath my feet now and I am looking up.

(And then there is a P. S., written later) God has directed me to a job. I got it. It's going to be tough for a while but I am going to make it all right, for I am God's child now. Some day I hope I am going to be able to meet you and tell you how all this was done.

From San Quentin Penitentiary: For the past two Sundays I have had the extreme pleasure of hearing your Old Fashioned Revival Hour and words cannot express the joy and comfort it brings here. I work in one of the few prison offices which enjoy the privileges of a radio. God willing, I shall continue to hear your program each Sunday night. I am truly thankful for a program such as yours, which brings Christ crucified to a sinsick world. Before getting into trouble which caused me to be here I did not know Christ as my Saviour, but in the Los Angeles county jail, while awaiting trial, I found Christ and was one of the first to be baptized there.

From the very first I desired to preach the Word. I had been here two months when I preached my first sermon. For the past year I have had no Christian fellowship and at times it has been hard to stand by myself, but I have found

His grace to be sufficient for all my difficulties. I try to always remember that it is the trying of our faith that is precious in His sight.

From British Columbia: Your Revival Hour has just finished and I want to thank God for the good listening to you has done to me. I was never clear on the word, "I have sinned," but now, through your enlightening and uplifting sermon, I see the whole picture. It has made me see myself, for I, too, was putting it off, saying there is yet time to ask for forgiveness. This wrong outlook is mine no more. I have sinned and will repent now. I am twenty-two years old and you are the first minister I ever listened to.

The gospel wrought this marvelous change: Just a few lines to let you know that we have been listening to your broadcast for the past three weeks. We sure are getting a blessing out of your sermons. We can hardly wait until Sunday night to hear another. I was saved once but I was an awful backslider. Three weeks ago tonight I was just getting over a drunk and fighting my family. I went over and turned on the radio and I heard your sermon through. I am happy to say that it brought me back to Christ. My wife and I are just getting along fine now, thanks to you and God. Praise the Lord.

Booze is my curse. I had company all Sunday afternoon and I was longing for them to go so I could rush the bucket for beer. While I was putting my coat on to go I turned on the radio and heard you. When you were finished I knelt and said, "Lord, I know you can take the desire away from me." I prayed good and hard for ten minutes. That bucket is not going tonight and I hope never again.

"A sinner, and a bad one" writes from Savannah, Georgia: I did not get your name and don't know whether you will get this or not. As I was dialing my radio I came across you. I have been in hell for a long time but your gospel tonight

woke me up. I am a sinner, and a bad one, but your gospel has done me good. I have hope now. You said to hope in Christ. I loved your song, "More About Jesus." I once was not so bad, but the devil got me. I would like to shake your hand and tell you that you did me good.

Mrs. Fuller tells the following story: After a broadcast, one Sunday evening, I was called to the telephone from the studio and there I heard a woman's sobbing voice saying, "Oh, I need help. I must have help. I need God!" I talked with her for a few minutes, but having another engagement I felt I could not go to her home, so I asked one of Mr. Fuller's secretaries who lived not far from her to go to see this woman in distress. This was her story:

She had been drinking and was slightly under the influence of liquor. She was ironing and the radio was on, playing jazz. This made her nervous and she walked to the radio to turn it off, but in turning the dial she said she heard a man's calm voice saying, "You have no peace! You need Christ!" And she thought, "That man is talking to me." So she left the radio on and listened throughout the sermon. Conviction gripped her heart and she felt her need of God. So she telephoned. Miss B. went to her home and dealt with her. As the Word of God penetrated through the stupor her face lit up and she made her decision for Christ.

From a prison in South Carolina: We listen to your program every Sunday night and wish to tell you just how much we enjoy the Old Fashioned Revival. Although we are not Christians it does our hearts so much good to hear your preaching from so far away. Mr. Fuller, we are in prison, but we want you and Mrs. Fuller to know that we can and do enjoy hearing the Word of God preached the way you preach it. We are both wanting to become Christians. We want you to pray for us that we may be saved. We also want you to send us the Heart-to-Heart Talks. We

217

assure you that they will be appreciated. Thank you in advance. We are your friends. (Signed by two men)

Saved from a drunkard's grave: I lost my wife four years ago and then I lost all, it seemed. I lost faith, hope and became despondent. I took to drinking, thinking it would help me to forget. It helped me to forget our dear Lord, to forget manhood, will power, and I am down as low as I think I could get without breaking all the commandments. I tried to get back. You don't know the trouble and misery I went through. I spent hours of prayers, tears and remorse. Time and time again I would fall back as the liquor habit and the devil had me down. I made a solemn promise that I would not give up, if death found me still seeking. Each time I came back I felt less worthy to ask the Lord to help. I became fearful lest He would turn against me and shut the door. Finally, after one of the parties that the devil had invited me to and I had accepted, I came to the conclusion that one of two things must happen. Either I must quit work and go to drinking as a business and get it over with or I must find the Lord.

Sunday evening, three weeks ago, I was listening to you on the radio and I started to wrestle with my troubles. I started out for liquor twice and came back with the firm determination to still seek the forgiving Lord. You were preaching on the only Door, Christ, and your words started me in a new line of thought. I commenced to see why I had not been able to get through the door. You said we must yield all. I had a little secret sin I did not wish to give up. I guess I thought I could hide it from God.

At last I got down on my knees and surrendered it all. Like a bolt out of the skies the Lord sent down His Spirit with forgiveness and I was saved. I was so happy that I threw out everything that pertained to liquor. From that minute to this I have not touched a drop and have no desire to touch it. I have lost all desire to do the things that I had been doing.

I have never been so happy as I have the last three weeks. The Lord has healed my soul, given me peace past my understanding and a new physical body—one that I have been trying to cure by medicine for the last five years. I feel so clean inside and out that I can't understand it. I am going to meet my dear mother, father and wife who died in the faith. It will not be long. I know this is a rather long recital but I had to thank you for showing me the way. God bless you. You are doing a wonderful work.

The happiest man in the world. I was saved under your ministry one year ago last Good Friday at Olympia Stadium in Detroit. This has been the greatest year in my life. Before I was saved, I was a terrible sinner. I was a drunkard and everything else, but the Lord Jesus Christ has made me a new creation. I am the happiest man in the world. I never dreamed that there was such peace and happiness to be had. How I do thank the dear Lord for saving my wicked soul. It is wonderful to know that Jesus never fails. (Signed "A sinner saved by grace.")

From a Michigan prison cell: I listen to your program of the Old time Revival Hour at every opportunity. I am very disappointed whenever it fails to reach me. I am an inmate in prison. I want you to know that there are a large number of men here who rejoice in the privilege of hearing the Word of God as you so graciously give it. I do not understand how anybody can turn aside and deny Christ after hearing your sermon. I have been studying for the past year for evangelistic work upon my release.

The beer went down the sink: I have had it on my mind to write you ever since last spring. I feel compelled to do so after hearing you over the radio tonight. Going back to the twentietn of March, I put in my Bible which I got the following week, "Born again," for your message, that memorable night, was on the twenty-third Psalm, "The Lord is my shepherd," and I accepted Him. I was not wholly sober at the time but the tears came and I fell on my knees and accepted Him. I poured the beer down the sink and I praise the Lord that He has kept me since. I gave up my pipe and snuff and tailor made cigarettes. May God bless you and your dear wife in your work.

Out of the gutter of sin: Three weeks ago I wrote you that I had listened to your program and had become a Christian. Each Sunday I have received new inspiration and, though my sins were scarlet, I am promised that they will be white as snow.

I called my mother who has prayed for me for twenty-five years, and now we listen together though we are far apart. Liquor ruined my life and brought me to the gutter. I was known to the police, and nothing else but the gospel could have saved me. I have returned to the church and attended both services today. My life, as I promised, will be spent to save others from now on. My wife is so happy. She feels that God has entered our home and will make it a happy one instead of a nightmare like it has been.

The singing is marvelous and takes me back to the days when my brother and sister, now dead, were a part of a trio which my good Baptist father and mother trained for church work.

From a California jail: I will write a few lines to let you know how we boys in this jail enjoy the wonderful radio program. I was committed to jail the thirty-first of July. I have turned on your dear program many times. There are about twenty men in this old high powered tank and about fourteen of them have given their hearts to God. Yes, this old jail is barred up awfully tight, but it just isn't tight enough to keep God's precious words out. Your voices come right in here to us. We boys are praying every night for God to make a way so that you can carry on and spread the old gospel.

A murderer awaiting execution: I noticed in your message, last Sunday night, you said people all over the U. S. A., Canada, the South Sea islands and South America could hear your message. I wondered if the thought came to your mind that many prisoners could hear also. God has provided a way so that we can receive the glorious gospel even in prison. Sunday night, seven of my brothers in Christ gathered around the radio here with me to listen to your message. It brought much gladness to our hearts, and as I saw them sitting there listening with their Bibles in their hands I greatly rejoiced over them, for the Lord has used me to lead them all to Him.

I was convicted of murder over a year ago and sentenced to death. I accepted Jesus as my personal Saviour the first day of September. I was baptized here at the county jail immediately afterward. I was the first prisoner ever to be baptized in the county jail. I have experienced the New Birth. God has transformed me into a new creature. My old sinful life has passed away and all things have become new. I have no desire for tobacco or anything that would be displeasing to God. He has given me peace beyond all understanding. I know by His Word that I have eternal life. I accepted His Word and have acted upon it. That has taken all the sting out of that death sentence which the court has imposed upon me.

I was a very vile person when I was sent here. I had gone down in sin to the uttermost and was almost an atheist. I thought the Bible was just a bunch of fables, but God has shown me differently. He had to strip me of everything I held dear before I would listen to His calling. I am so thankful today that He did. Had He not, I would still be in my sins. Heaven is worth any price we pay for it. It seemed very bitter at first, but since I have learned to understand God's Word it has turned out to be as sweet as honey. I have no regrets that I am here. It is just like going to school. I spend most of my time reading the Bible. I have a wonderful Bible teacher. She comes to the jail twice a week and teaches for two hours. Her marvelous teaching has taught me to seek and love God with all my heart.

These men in jail are easy to lead to the Lord. Most of them are in deep trouble. It is easy to show them that sin does not pay and that the devil is a very poor paymaster. We prisoners know that the world will not forgive us for our mistakes, but God has forgiven us. I am enclosing a dollar to help meet your need on the network.

A second letter from a Kansas listener: You will recall having received a letter of heart breaking failure from me a short while ago. Tonight I have a different story. I have been under terrible conviction since writing you that letter. I was in the county jail when I received your first book. That Sabbath morning I was in a most dreadful state of mind. Finally, I read two wonderful chapters of a book that a dear lady sent me from California. It suddenly broke through that He was able to save even a boy like me, and that He was able to keep me. I asked Him to help me. I got out pencil and paper and counted some of the cost. Then praying as I went, I started for the stables. I climbed into the loft, knelt down behind some hay and there Jesus Christ came into my heart. At first I just walked back and forth across the loft and praised the Lord. Oh, Mrs. Fuller, I have such a blessed peace tonight. It is wonderful to walk with my hand in His and with my eyes straining upward for His approving smile, for I must not take my eyes off Him.

I have already started over the road of restitution. Please pray that I may remain true. I wish to thank you and all the faithful Christians for your prayers. Thanks so much for the nice books you sent me. My whole life is being built on this Scripture, "For I know whom I have believed, and am persuaded that He is able to keep that which I have committed unto Him against that day." P. S. Please send me all the Scripture and doctrine possible on restitution.

A real penitent in the penitentiary: While sitting here in my death cell, I count it a joyful privilege in writing to you as a Christian brother. A lady in California sent me books to read, also a Bible and religious literature, and now I find that, through her, I am on your mailing list and am receiving the Keys to the Scripture and the Heart-to-Heart Talks. I am thanking God for her kindness in sending me these papers and when I pass on to be with Jesus I will take a great load of love for Christian friends who have been so good to me.

I wish that I might be able to live only to work for the glory of our Lord. Please remember me in your prayers. I have been confined in the death cell forty-two months. Even though I did wrong and came short of the glory of God, as many young men do, the merciful Saviour has forgiven me for my part in that awful crime and I am praying for all that I sinned against in this world, that they will have mercy too. I would love to have the liberty to explain my case and pass the light on to other young men, poor mothers' boys who followed after the things that old Satan had to offer them, which may lead them to the death cell if they continue on the downward path and the way to destruction, as I did.

The writer had to sink into the very depths of sin before crying to God for mercy. Yes, I went from a worldly social position to the gutter, and there I found I had no place to sleep, nothing to eat, travelled in box cars from one part of the country to another, but now your gospel Hour has been like a beacon light directing me to God and I have now found Christ as a friend and a joy that I had never dreamed of. Today I am back with my dear wife. We have happiness and contentment we never knew before by the wonderful grace of God.

I am not much at writing, but I must tell you a little of what you have done for me as I have listened. It would be impossible to tell all. I have just buried myself in this little town on the New England coast and for nearly eighteen years have earned my living by fishing. When I was young I got on the wrong path for a while and committed an awful crime. I was not found out, but I often wished I had been, for the years of remorse have been terrible to bear. It wasn't murder, but it was something terrible and it seemed there was no way for me to make it right. None of my folks know where I am and my only companion is my black cat. I call him "Snowball" or "Snowy" for short. I have a radio and, one night last winter, I happened to get your program clear as a bell, though it was storming and sleeting outside. I drank in every word you said and you said plenty about how a sinner could come to the Saviour and have forgiveness, and that was what I longed for. I grasped every word and all week, while mending nets or bringing in fish, I would go over and over what you told from the Bible and I kept listening in. To make the story short, I will tell you that another stormy Sunday night I was listening to you and I just felt God was right there with me, and I got down on my knees and talked to Him like a friend. And this is what you quoted while I was there crying some (and I haven't shed a tear before in years), "Though your sins be as scarlet, they shall be as white as snow." And, praise God, that is true, for Christ paid the penalty for that awful sin I committed and God has forgiven and forgotten. I am so happy!

I was so discouraged, Sunday night, that I could hardly see my way out, but turning my radio on I got you and your program. The singing was beautiful and the message from God's Word helped me so much. I have been a Christian and do know it is the only way to be happy. My husband and I were so happy in the past, but we both began to drink and the first thing we knew we were back in sin. Oh, how easy it is to drink unless we do live close to the Lord. To-day we are separated, not divorced, and I am so unhappy. I want to continue to listen to your program.

21

THE AREAS OF ISOLATION AND LONESOMENESS

IT IS almost beyond our power to realize that not a person in the United States is living in a section too remote to be within range of the Old Fashioned Revival Hour provided the listener has a good radio set. But this is not all. Canada, Alaska, Hawaii, the South Sea islands, portions of Central and South America, the West Indies, and even more remote sections of the world are listening in. Farther and farther, by means of short wave, this gospel program is reaching out literally to all the world.

Those who live in the midst of churches and friends, enjoying every opportunity for Christian fellowship, can scarcely conceive of the hunger for human companionship of those buried in the mountain and desert regions, far from gospel services. To them a friendly hand is extended every Sunday evening as they are welcomed to the great circle of Christians. Heartache and loneliness are forgotten. If there are tears they are tears of joy over the opportunity to forget, for a little while, the burdens which press in upon them.

From the West Indies: Far away in this remote island, over three hundred and seventy-five persons listened to your program Sunday afternoon. Hearts have been glad to hear those familiar songs and receive the inspiration of your messages.

Dear Mr. Fuller: I am an old miner living alone up in the hills in a little shack where I can see way out over the valley. It would be awful lonesome if I didn't have my dog, Shep, who is getting pretty old, and my burro Baldy.

I usually get your program pretty good on my little radio and I sure do enjoy it. I was raised religious, but it has been many a year since I went to a church. I have lived a very careless life, kinda forgot God a good many years until I've been listening to your talks about the Bible. I got a little Bible out of an old box where it has been a long, long time. My mother gave it to me when I was a little boy and I am going to read it now, every day. You explain it so I can understand what you are talking about. When you sang "What A Friend We Have In Jesus," it took me back quite a piece for my mother used to sing that song as she worked around the house. She was a widow and she sure needed a friend. She knew the Lord like a friend. It seems like I was back a little shaver again and my brother and sister were there and mother singing to us. She was a good mother. I never thought that I would be a lonesome old miner, not much good to anybody. Yes, old Shep and me are awaiting for you every Sunday night to tell us some more about the Bible. I ask the Lord to forgive my many sins of the past and make my heart clean so I'll be ready.

A man writes from Mexico and he says: I heard your gospel broadcast and I want you to know my appreciation for the messages that have come to me on the subject of our soul's salvation. You have answered all my own problems, as if you preached to me personally. Here in this country one cannot find the true gospel, for churches of that type are so far apart, so you can understand what your radio broadcast means to me, who am thirsting after the waters of life.

From Honolulu: I would like to be one of the first to offer sincere congratulations on the excellence of your radio program and to tell you that the reception is so fine out here in Honolulu that it seems as though you are speaking in the room. Your inspirational talk of last Sunday night is something I shall never forget.

From a cook on an isolated western ranch: I have found God through your ministry and shall never turn away from Him. I am so happy now. I have lived a wasted life. I do not know as much about the Bible as a ten year old child, but I am going to learn. I must put all my spare time into learning. I cook on a ranch out in the country and never get to go to church. I have not been in a church for about nine years. God has blessed my little radio and through the message has saved me. I am so hungry to hear more I can hardly wait from one Sunday to the next.

From Alaska: Your broadcast came in well again last Sunday night. There were thirteen of us here listening in. I wish you could have seen the faces of the young people present and their eagerness to learn more of God's Word. There were eighteen present at our little service that followed. We could feel the Lord's presence and knew He was dealing with souls. There were others in the village who were tuned in on their own radios last Sunday night.

From Pecan Island, Louisiana: I live sixty-five miles from the nearest town and six miles from the Gulf of Mexico. I have two boys, one ten and one thirteen years old. Neither one can walk a step. I am a world war veteran, seventy percent disabled, so you can see that my cross is pretty heavy to bear. I look forward to your Sunday night services. They are such a blessing to me. I am glad to make a real sacrifice and send my little bit to help.

From Nassau, in the Bahamas: We listen to your program here. It comes in very clearly, and we hope it will continue, as it surely revives our spirits.

From a lonely ranch in Colorado: In my lonely mountain cabin, forty-five miles from any railroad, I have just listened to your blessed Hour. Life in these mountains, with the snow two and one half feet deep on the level, would be all but unbearable except for my little battery set which brings to me, every Sunday night, the voices of your fine singers and your wonderful messages. This week I have a letter from my aged mother down in Tennessee. She told me that she, too, listens every Sunday night. Your service tonight brought me nearer to Christ and to my dear old mother, for I knew that she was listening to the same voices and the same comforting words of God as you spoke them.

Nantucket Light Ship: I thought I would write and let you know that your message not only goes from Alaska to Panama and from coast to coast but one hundred miles out in the Atlantic Ocean off of Cape Cod to the Nantucket Light Ship. I am one of the sailors on this ship. We stay out here two months at a time without once seeing land, but I thank God at least once a week I can hear the true message of the redeeming blood of our Lord Jesus Christ.

The Mountain People of Kentucky listen: I am a railroad man and being away from home a great deal I don't get to hear you every Sunday night. Last Sunday night I was at home and enjoyed your program very much with my family, which listens regularly. Your sermons are a great inspiration to me and mine, as well as to thousands of other mountain folks in the rural sections in these great hills. Hundreds upon hundreds of the mountain people who are deprived of the privilege of going to church are getting your messages and it brings food to their hungry hearts. Much comment is made, in this section, of your great work.

Here is a letter from Newfoundland: I live in a lonely outpost on the island of Newfoundland and listen to your wonderful program every Sunday night. I find it most inspiring. We have winter here now with about four feet of snow and a temperature of about twenty below zero. Sometime ago I attended a very unique service here at which a group of sailors from the United States fleet provided the program. It was a group of twenty seamen belonging to a prayer circle led by a young man. The boys sang and gave testimony to their conversion and the keeping power of Christ. One was a tall, husky Texan who told of his very recent conversion which he attributed to listening to the Charles Fuller broadcast heard on the battleship. If you could have seen this big fellow and heard him speak, Mr. Fuller, you would surely have felt repaid for all your efforts. I, for one, felt so moved that the tears were streaming down my face. There was a hush over the great audience as he spoke. The big sailor, in closing his glorious testimony, stepped forward and sang in a ringing tenor voice, "Rock of Ages."

From a log cabin in the southland: Nestled in the lonesome hills of Mississippi in a humble log cabin, our family of twelve always listen and find comfort and restoration of spirit in your beautiful music and glowing words about Christ our Saviour.

From a missionary in Venezuela, S. A.: I just want to let you know that way down here in Central Venezuela, South America, we are able to get your Revival Hour through the Hawaiian Islands. It was quite a thrill the night that we first picked you up. What a treat it is after one comes home tired from the evening service to sit down and drink in those inspiring songs, to hear the old time message of salvation and to know that it is going out over the air through so many stations and just blanketing North America.

From the islands of Puget Sound: I have listened to your broadcast for almost a year. I rejoice that your sound gospel messages are reaching the out-of-the-way places. In the section where I live, in northwestern Washington, 140,000 people live in small settlements in the mountains on the shores of Puget Sound and on thirty-one islands of the San Juan Island groups. There, many live and die without hearing a single gospel message. The boat men and fishermen are on the waters day after day. Many of them are never ashore long enough to attend a church service. My heart has been nearly broken as I have thought of them. I believe your gospel service reaches many of these people on the water and in the little cabins high in the mountains and that, as they listen in, many are hearing of Christ for the first time. How I long for them all to accept the Christ who has transformed my life.

A good letter from Newfoundland: This is to let you know that we hear you away over here on North Chains Island. It is about one and a quarter miles long and about a quarter of a mile wide. It was a glorious message received here at eleven o'clock tonight, Christmas Eve. We missed the very first part but picked you up when you were singing that great song, "For He is So Precious to Me," and we sang with you. We certainly are having our winter snows and frosts and are frozen up until some time in April. Then we will be free again to move about in our motor boats and steamers, making their usual weekly calls with mail and freight. During the winter months we get our mail by dog team over the ice which at times is dangerous, but we have never had any serious accidents or a loss of life, for which we are thankful.

From a U. S. Battleship in Pearl Harbor, T. H.: A group of service men, army and navy, gather together every Sunday to hear your message and we are certainly uplifted by it and receive such a blessing by hearing the Word of God preached over the air. I pray every day for your work and am enclosing a little to help. I wish it were more.

My husband is superintendent of a mining camp far up in the mountains. We are snowed in for seven months and I do not know how I could get along without your services. The mine runs Sundays and there is nothing but my radio to make the day any different from any other day, so I always look forward to your broadcast.

From Arizona: We do enjoy the broadcasts and can hardly wait from one Sunday to the next. Our radio battery was down this last Sunday night, so we drove six miles over to another old couple's house to hear your sermon and the wonderful singing, and listened all together to the songs we used to hear when we were children. Your broadcast is such a blessing to the old folks and invalids. We are an old couple living at the foot of the White Mountains in Arizona.

From Soldiers at Fort Randolph in the Canal Zone: We have been listening to your talks nearly every Sunday and they have certainly been interesting to us. We are writing this to let you know how much we have appreciated them. We are from various parts of the States and will be listening to you from Panama on your future broadcasts.

From a one-room cabin: We live in a little one-room cabin out in the sage brush desert near Caldwell, Idaho, and we can pick up your Old Fashioned Revival Hour clearly. Your messages have gripped my heart. Maybe you can imagine what they mean to us out here.

From Honolulu: I want to write to you and let you know

what a joy it is to tune in and hear your program way over here in Honolulu. We moved from Kansas because my husband is an army man and was transferred here. You can never realize what it meant to us when we tuned in, Sunday, and could hear you again, just as we did at home. Everybody asked me why I cried and I said, "These are just tears of joy," for I never dreamed that we could get our beloved broadcast here. It was like having an old friend walk into our living room. There are lots of people over here that are far away from home and depend on your broadcast.

Another letter from Honolulu: We want you to know how blessed it was to hear the message of the Old Fashioned Revival Hour again. The music was very beautiful and the reception as clear as it was at home on the coast. This Hour is truly a bond that draws so many widely separated sections together and unless you get far from home you can't really know what it means.

When the battery doesn't go dead: We live on a little farm on dirt roads, quite a ways from any church, but we have our radio so we can get the Old Fashioned Revival Hour, if our battery has enough juice. Last night it went down just as the service was over. We were so glad it lasted till it was over. We don't have much to send but want to do our bit to help and we hope there will be a way provided for us to get our battery charged so we can get the service next Sunday night. We tell people, yes everyone we meet, to listen in, too.

From New Mexico: My husband and I live in the mountains of New Mexico and have no other chance of worship. Since we cannot go to church we look forward to your Sunday night broadcast and enjoy every moment of the Hour. We wish it was on every day of the week.

A woman writes from Honduras: Your program is a great blessing to me. It is beautiful to feel included in a great circle, to worship and sing God's praise and hear the Word expounded so sincerely.

A Massachusetts woman writes: Only the other day I received a letter from a missionary in Central America. They said that they heard your broadcast and were so pleased with it.

A Christian sailor boy: I sure enjoy your broadcasts whenever I have an opportunity to listen in. Christ is my life and light and there is nothing like having Him for an every day friend even aboard a battleship. I trust many souls will be saved as God calls men to anchor their souls in His fathomless love.

From Alberta, Canada: We are so glad that your services come to us, away up here, and we are thankful we can hear you clearly on Sundays. Hubby must hurry and get the cows milked and I must leave my supper dishes, if not done, so we can listen. We have no church or service of any kind near here, so the dear old hymns you sing take me back to my childhood days in England when we had cottage meetings and Sunday school in our home. I would like a picture of you all. Just now I have no money in the house, as we came only a few years ago from a dried out district where we lost everything. We are having a hard time, but are trusting God.

From the Canal Zone: I am praying that you will never have to go off the air, for we humans cannot measure the results that are being accomplished. I wish I could tell you all the good things I hear about you here in the Canal Zone and about the large numbers that are listening, increasingly large numbers, but the time will not permit and, some day, you will know. To God be all the glory, and may He richly bless all who have any part whatever in putting forth the unadulterated Word of God.

From a ranch in Colorado: We live on a timber ranch up

in the foothills of the eastern slope of the Rockies and we look forward to your blessed program. We have a wind driven battery charger up on a mountain (the wind doesn't blow hard enough down here in the valley) and I have the job of carrying a "dead" battery up and a recharged one down in order to get to listen to you, but it is more than worth the effort. We enjoy so much the excellent sermons of Rev. Fuller, the letter reading of Mrs. Fuller, the unbeatable singing of the quartet and choir and the masterful playing of your pianist.

From a young home missionary working among the seamen in the northwest: Here in the Olympics and in the boats of Puget Sound there are many who never are able to attend church. We have met many who say they listen to the Old Fashioned Revival Hour and are under deep conviction. I wanted to write you to keep up the good work, by all means. Oh, if you could only see these hungry people! I just thank God that you are on the air and are reaching these places that are totally unreached. I would love to live long enough to reach every home in America, just to be sure that they have heard the story of redemption at least one time. The radio can reach every home and I just hope your program may. If you should ever become doubtful as to the amount of real soul winning your program does, just remember that in an area of 7,087 square miles of a last American frontier many listening ears are tuned in.

From the Bad Lands of North Dakota: Picture us—we have a little, old sod house, one story high, with everything old and worn. A tall, thin man over fifty years of age, a wife tiny and frail and their son twenty-four years old sitting around the radio, waiting with bated breath while someone dials eagerly to get Brother and Sister Fuller way off in Los Angeles. My, how we do enjoy your sermons, music, prayers and letters. The radio is a marvelous invention to spread the gospel to isolated places, and this surely is one of them. We live in the heart of the bad lands of North Dakota, in the grasshopper and drought devastated country. Even though we have had to dispose of most of our cattle and horses and a couple of sections of land, yet God has blessed us in a wonderful, glorious way. In the past six years, while material blessings have diminished to almost nothing (even household utensils are all holes and mends) yet we are rejoicing in the spoiling of our goods, for God has been a Real Presence and we are continually looking up and rejoicing in Him.

From a sheep ranch in Montana: You are the only one we have ever heard who thinks of the sheep herder. God bless you for it. We have a sheep ranch out here on the prairie. My husband has a radio in his sheep wagon. We would just like to thank you very much for the many blessings we have had while hearing you over the radio. You don't know what it means to us to have such a fine program coming right into our sheep wagon, out here on the lonely prairies.

Thirty-five miles from church: Our family looks forward to the Sunday night service, for we live away out in the mountains and the nearest church is thirty-five miles away and over bad roads. We have much snow in the winter.

From another mountain home: I know it would do your heart good if you could look into some of these homes and tent houses tucked away in the mountains and see families and neighbors gathered in, listening to your program. You can never know on this earth the souls you are reaching through these broadcasts or what it means to us to hear the music and the preaching. We look forward to it all the week.

From a gold mining camp in Idaho: My husband was a

minister but it pleased God to take him home a few weeks ago, to leave me lonely and our babe fatherless. Two weeks ago I came into this gold mining camp to teach school. The snow is so deep I cannot see out of my school room windows. People and mail come and go only by airplane. These two Sundays are only the beginning of many Sundays where there is no church or Sunday school. Your services are going to mean much, and already every word and note I've heard seem to be just for me. Many times, in these dark, trying hours of sorrow and loneliness, when I could not even pray, I have merely whispered, "Lord Jesus, I love you still and, like Job, if you slay me I'll trust you still."

I am left with many, many bills to pay, two hundred miles from my darling little one who is with her grandmother. I suffer bitter pangs of loneliness and life seems to hold so little for me. But Heaven is so near. God is so real. His promise is true and He has walked by my side, suffering every pang I feel. He constantly assures me that if I'll only trust Him He can work out His plan and purpose to one beautiful end. Some day I'll understand.

From Sonora, Mexico: We are living in a little Mexican mining camp, seventy miles from Douglas, Arizona. We are the only Americans here. We used to listen to your service in California. We were isolated from church fellowship there but here very much more so. We do thank God, with you, for the many lonely hearts you reach and comfort through God's Word and spiritual songs.

From an aged brother in the State of Washington: I trust you will not think me presumptuous in calling you brother, but you have, indeed, been a brother to me during the time I have had the privilege of hearing you for the past few months. I do not know just how to thank you for the help and blessing I have had. It is impossible for you to understand the position I am in today—and have been for the past few years. Sometimes I have felt that I have been forsaken by my Lord whom I have been trying to serve for many years. But when I give the matter a second thought I well know He does not forsake anyone. I am isolated from everything that I have been used to in the past forty years. I am now living away out on a "stump-brush ranch" working for my board under a very harsh boss. It seems harder for me because I once was rather prosperous and enjoyed some comforts of life. A fire completely wiped me out,— home, drug store and everything including a Bible I had owned for fifty years. Well, when such fine music and good news comes from you as I have been hearing it makes me feel like I am not completely forgotten. Just thirty more days and I will reach my seventy-second milestone. There is not a sound that comes over the radio that is as plain and distinct as your voice. Several times during the service I have shed some bitter tears, but I suppose tears are honorable when shed for joy.

From a remote Montana town: You just seem like old friends to us. I am just sure we will know you when we meet in Heaven. When Brother Fuller spoke in Chicago we listened in, with the rest, sang the songs and prayed. Anyone outside our cabin would have thought we were crazy. Maybe we were, crazy with joy to be able to pick up such a sermon. When two old people, well up in their sixties, are all alone up in the mountains, radio people are alive and real to them.

Others listen, too, in Alabama: We surely do enjoy your program every Sunday night and we have been telling our friends and neighbors and inviting them in, and sometimes we have as many as twenty or twenty-five people packed here in our sitting room.

A letter from Kentucky: The teacher of the adult Bible class announced at Sunday school that we would have church service that evening at 7:00 o'clock and that the services would be conducted by the Rev. Charles E. Fuller of Los Angeles, Calif. At the appointed time the radio was brought to church and we tuned in for your blessed Hour. It came through clear as could be. Everyone present enjoyed the entire program very much. At the close, prayer was offered thanking God for the privilege that we had of enjoying your program and prayers went up to God that you might not have to go off the air. We certainly enjoy every broadcast, Sunday evening, and we have a radio in the barn and hear you preach while we are milking. We have a dairy, and milking time comes just as your broadcast comes on.

A lonely miner in Nevada: Two weeks ago tonight I was alone at our mining camp, fifty miles from town and high on a mountain. The camp is so remote and inaccessible that we pack in with burros. A certain party who was to pack in with me that particular night was unable to go, so I had to pack in alone, arriving at camp after dark.

Just the day before we had laid away, in the little desert cemetery here, my aunt who has lived with us for forty-one years and who was as close to me as my own mother. Although we knew for a certainty she was with her Lord in glory, yet her passing was hard to bear. So you can imagine how lonely and depressed I was that night alone there on that high mountain.

However, about an hour after arriving at camp I turned on our battery radio in order to hear your broadcast, and as the Lord so willed it you preached that night on the certainty of the resurrection of those who die in the Lord. I can't describe to you how quickly the burden of grief was lifted. In just a few minutes I was joining with the choir and quartet in those inspirational resurrection songs. May I take this opportunity of thanking you for that splendid sermon. The Lord through you gave me just what I needed that night.

Lonely folks in Montana: The past three Sundays are the first we have heard your messages for a long time. My Brother, we are so hungry for God's Word. Haven't heard a sermon in seven months. A minister came nearly one hundred miles to preach for us then. Oh, how it revived us. Last Tuesday's mail (mail comes on Tuesdays and Fridays) brought a letter from my niece. She enclosed a dollar bill and wrote, "Buy yourselves some candy or something you are specially hungry for." *Our* old hearts are so hungry for the Word of God. So I says that dollar goes to Brother Fuller for giving us the Word. We do enjoy your literature. Please pray for our unsaved loved ones, and pray for us that we may be faithful.

22

A LAST WORD ABOUT THE BROADCAST

A SYNDICATED NEWSPAPER column entitled "Washington Day by Day," published in more than three hundred eastern newspapers, paid the following tribute:

"In a world with war and crime writing the annals of greed and violence in the blood of countless victims, it is restful to hear an old-fashioned preacher preach old-time religion in the good old-fashioned way. Coming out of California every Sunday evening, this gospel hour of the radio breaks through the din and clamor of swing-whoopee, croonings, and news broadcasts to almost startle a weary world with its unretouched truths.

"This earnest, pleading Baptist preacher who exhorts a bizarre world in a manner simple and devoid of sophism is the Rev. Charles E. Fuller, and he gives his address as Box 123, Los Angeles. His millions of devoted listeners contribute the money for buying radio time on 120 stations—a whole hour each week—indubitably a stupendous sum.

"The radio sets of blasé Washingtonians pick Evange-list Fuller's soul-searching messages from the gentle autumn breezes that blow out of the night across Potomac lushlands and over the low-hung islands which dot historic Chesapeake Bay. The congregation's singing of such time-tried hymns as 'Fountain Filled with Blood,' 'Let the Lower Lights be Burning,' and 'Sweet Hour of Prayer,' comes like a ground swell from a new and better world, and by the air waves reaches comforting hands across all the North American continent and to the islands of the sea, bringing the new-old story of religion to the weary heart not only here in sophisticated Washington, but to mansions and hovels, homes and brothels, prisons and cocktail lounges the country over. It steals into rooms made restless by the unquiet slumber of sick life, hovers over the cabins in the cotton belt and filters into the lumbermen's camps of the great North woods."

Mr. R. H. Alber of the Alber Company handles for Mr. Fuller the enormous work of placing this evangelistic feature and contracting for it with the various radio stations and broadcasting systems.

The broadcast covers by far the largest number of stations of any program regularly on the air, either commercial or religious, far outstripping such commercial releases as Amos 'n' Andy, Texaco Corporation, Ford Symphony Hour, and others. This is truly a testimony to the power of the Gospel. God is certainly blessing the Old Fashioned Revival Hour in a wonderful way.

Mail is constantly received from listeners in China, the

Philippines, New Zealand, Australia, all sections of South America, Africa, and many other foreign countries—from listeners who eagerly look forward to its weekly inspiration.

POSTLUDE

W<small>E SHOULD</small> like to close this recital of the mercy and
goodness of God and of the lives of two whom mil-
lions love, with a glimpse of that life beyond which we
confidently know awaits us and all others who love the
Lord Jesus Christ. We have chosen for this a letter which
was sent in answer to the announcement by Mr. Fuller
that the following Sunday evening he would speak on
Heaven. The letter was written by an old man who was
very ill. Here it is, in part:

"Next Sunday you are to talk about Heaven. I am interested in that land, because I have held a clear title to a
bit of property there for over fifty-five years. I did not
buy it. It was given to me without money and without
price. But the donor, Jesus Christ, purchased it for me at
tremendous sacrifice. I am not holding it for speculation
since the title is not transferable. It is not a vacant lot.

"For more than half a century I have been sending ma-
terials out of which the greatest architect and builder of the
universe has been building a home for me, which will never

244

need to be remodeled nor repaired because it will suit me perfectly, individually, and will never grow old. Termites can never undermine its foundations, for they rest upon the Rock of Ages. Fire cannot destroy it. Floods cannot wash it away. No locks nor bolts will ever be placed upon its doors, for no vicious persons can ever enter that land where my dwelling stands, now almost completed and ready for me to enter in and abide in peace eternally, without fear of being ejected.

"There is a valley of deep shadows between the place where I live in California and that to which I shall journey in a very short time. I cannot reach my home in that city of gold without passing through this dark valley of shadows. But I am not afraid, because the best friend I ever had, my Saviour, went through the same valley long, long ago and drove away all its gloom. He has stuck by me through thick and thin since we first became acquainted fifty-five years ago, and I hold His promise in printed form, never to forsake me nor to leave me alone. He will be with me as I walk through the valley of shadows, and I shall not lose my way when He is with me.

"I hope to hear your sermon on Heaven next Sunday, but I have no assurance that I shall be able to do so. My ticket to Heaven has no date marked for the journey—no return coupon—and no permit for baggage. Yes, I am all ready to go, and I may not be here while you are talking next Sunday evening, but I shall meet you there some day, through the riches of grace in Jesus Christ."

HOW TO BE SAVED

It is fitting that this account of the greatest of all gospel broadcasts should not end without a definite and simply stated explanation of the way of salvation.

If you, dear reader, do not have the assurance of your salvation, will you just now ask the Holy Spirit to enlighten your heart, in order that you may know for yourself the peace which has come to those who have given testimony in the letters you have read.

First of all, you must know that you are a sinner and that you cannot save yourself. God's Word says, "All have sinned and come short of the glory of God," Romans 3:23. That includes you. There are no exceptions.

Secondly, you must realize that God loves you and has made provision for you to be guiltless in His sight, in spite of your sins. "But God commendeth His love toward us, in that, while we were yet sinners, Christ died for us," Romans 5:8. "As ye have yielded your members servants to uncleanness and to iniquity unto iniquity; even so now yield your members servants to righteousness unto holiness," Romans 6:19.

Thirdly, you must be convinced that in the atonement of Jesus Christ, God's only begotten Son, which He wrought on the cross when He died there as your sin-bearer, is your only way of escape from judgment. "Without the shedding of blood is *no* remission," Hebrews 9:22. "Neither is there salvation in any other: for there is *none other name* under heaven, given among men, whereby we *must* be saved," Acts 4:12. "Believe on the Lord Jesus Christ and thou shalt be saved," Acts 16:31. "How shall we escape, if we neglect so great salvation," Hebrews 2:3.

Fourthly, you must trust Him as your *personal* Saviour, committing your life to Him and inviting Him to come into your heart by His Spirit, bringing to you the Saviour's precious gift of eternal life. This wonderful gift is provided for every member of the human race, but only those who take it by a definite act of faith receive it.

May I illustrate. Let us suppose that the government of the United States provides a home with ten acres of land and a monthly income of $100 to every person who, on the first day of January, visits the office of the town or city clerk and files an application for these benefits.

A certain number appear on the appointed day and file the application as required. Thereupon the government, as promised, issues the deed and a check for $100 for the first monthly installment on the pension.

Certain others do not go until about the middle of January. They are informed that they are too late. Others, instead of filing the required application, bring an affidavit stating that they pay their bills promptly and have never been convicted of a crime. They, too, are turned down. They have chosen not to meet the simple conditions laid down for receiving the reward.

God has the right to insist on the requirements which His wisdom and justice have ordained. He says, "Whosoever believeth in Him (the Lord Jesus Christ) should not perish, but have everlasting life," John 3:16. He holds out the gift of eternal life to you under these conditions, and these conditions alone. When you come to Him professing to have goodness or merit of your own He will not receive you. YOU MUST MEET HIS CONDITIONS.

Fifthly, to be a victorious Christian you must make it the first business of your life to know and do His will. This will not be a hardship but a great joy, because you will love Him more and more as you realize how wonderful is His love and how adequate is His provision for your need, whatever that may be. There are three indispensable requirements for living an overcoming Christian life. First, the habitual, daily study of God's Word, in order that you may become acquainted with Him by treasuring in your heart His words to you. "Thy Word have I hid in my heart, that I might not sin against Thee," Psalm 119:11. "Study to show thyself approved unto God, a workman that needeth not to be ashamed, rightly dividing the word of truth," II Timothy 2:15.

Then, by talking with Him and letting Him speak to you directly by His Spirit, who is sent to be your Instructor, Guide and Comforter. "But the Comforter, which is the Holy Ghost, whom the Father will send in my name, He shall teach you all things, and bring all things to your remembrance, whatsoever I have said unto you," John 14:26.

Also, by becoming His witness to others at every opportunity. You will grow spiritually as you share with others this knowledge of Him which has changed your own life. "Ye are my witnesses," Isa. 43:10. "He (Andrew) *first findeth his own brother* Simon, and saith unto him, we have found the . . . Christ," John 1:41.

My decision

Confessing myself to be sinful and deserving of God's judgment, but believing that Jesus Christ, God's only begotten Son, paid the penalty for my sins upon Calvary, I do now accept Him as my Lord and Saviour and receive from Him the gift of eternal life which He offers. I give to Him my heart and life from this time forth.

Name_____

Address_____

Prayer

Dear heavenly Father:

We trust Thee just now to reveal Thyself to this needy heart who has come to Thee in humble confession. May Thy Holy Spirit cleanse away all sin by the application of the atoning blood of the Saviour and may the witness of the Spirit be given that the transaction is done in accordance with Thy promise. In Jesus' name, Amen.

> " 'Tis done: the great transaction's done;
>   I am my Lord's, and He is mine;
> He drew me and I followed on,
>   Charmed to confess the voice divine.
>
> Happy day, happy day, when Jesus washed my
>   sins away!
>   He taught me how to watch and pray,
>   And live rejoicing ev'ry day;
> Happy day, happy day, when Jesus washed my
>   sins away."

HEART TO HEART TALK.

MY GREETING.

I thought to wish that God might truly bless you;
But that, I see, He's clearly bound to do:
He is Himself the fountain of all blessing,
And loves to bless His children -- therefore you!

I thought to wish that for your earthly journey
God would supply your need: (could He forget?):
But now I see that He has clearly promised
To meet all need -- and so it shall be met!

Then I might ask that God Himself might guide you;
But this is needless, since He is your Guide:
Since He has promised constantly to guide us
Until we reach, at last, the Other Side.

What shall I ask then, -- what indeed is left me;
What say to gladden as you journey here;
How can I help to comfort, strengthen, hearten,
As you tread nobly through each passing year?

How can I -- save that, gently, I remind you
Being His child you are supremely blest:
And that whate'er may come -- of joy or sorrow --
All that He gives or sends is aye the BEST.
                                -- J. Danson Smith.

"And the Lord went before them by day in a pillar of cloud,
to lead them the way; and by night in a pillar of fire, to give
them light; to go by day and night" -- Ex. 13:21.

"Jesus never sends a man ahead alone. He blazes a clear
way through every thicket and woods, and then softly calls,
"Follow me. Let's go on together, you and I." He has been
everywhere that we are called to go. His feet have trodden down
smooth a path through every experience that comes to us. He
knows each road, and knows it well: the valley road of disappointment with its dark shadows; the steep road of temptation down
through the rocky ravines and slippery gullies; the narrow path
of pain, with the brambly thorne bushes so close on each side,
with their slash and sting; the dizzy road along the heights of
victory; the old beaten road of commonplace daily routine. EVERY
DAY PATHS HE HAS TRODDEN AND GLORIFIED, AND WILL WALK ANEW WITH

REDUCED FACSIMILE

2

EACH OF US. THE ONLY SAFE WAY TO TRAVEL IS WITH HIM ALONGSIDE AND IN CONTROL." -- S. D. Gordon.

Did you hear the King of England give his Christmas broadcast? If you did you never will forget his closing words, "I said to the man who stood at the gate of the year, 'Give me a light that I may tread safely into the unknown.' He said, 'Go forth into the dark, and put your hand into the hand of God. That shall be to you better than light and safer than a known way.'"

"The supernatural always slumbers when faith lies sleeping or dead."

"Men ought always to pray and not to faint" -- Luke 18:1. That little "ought" is emphatic. It implies obligation as high as Heaven. Jesus said, "men ought ALWAYS to pray" and added "and NOT TO FAINT."

I confess I do not always FEEL like praying -- when, judging by my feelings, there is no one listening to my prayer. And then these words have stirred me to pray

I OUGHT to pray --
I ought ALWAYS to pray --
I SHOULD NOT GROW FAINT in praying.

"Then ye pray -- BELIEVE" -- Mark 11:24.

O, may He OVERTAKE us, as the path of life we tread!
Along our way of sorrow may His radiant Light be shed....
O may He come to warm the heart and ease the heavy load --
And walk with us as long ago He walked the Emmaus road.

Take the road ... the lonely road -- courageous, unafraid!
Ready for the journey when the twilight shadows fade...
God whose Love is Omnipresent -- will He fail us then? --
Or forget the covenant that He has made with men?
-- Patience Strong.

"The God of the infinite is the God of the infinitesimal."

"If you can't pray -- worry."

3

Dear friends, "That I may know His" -- that is my prayer for this new year, for it covers everything. That I pray for myself I pray for each one of you! Christianity is moving a Person -- not adhering to a complex set of rules. Christianity is a living faith in a living Christ. May we come to KNOW HIM in His fulness in this new year. He died for us -- may we live for Him.

The race has been a long one. I feel that we are now in the last lap. Let us press on in prayer, in Bible study, conserving and using our energies for Him, that in coming "to know Him" we may make His known.

Only God knows what the harvest has been in the past year -- the number of souls which were hell-bound, and are now joyfully pressing Heaven-ward because you have been faithful, and as a result the Holy Spirit has been enabled to use God's Word as it has gone out over the radio, carrying the good news of salvation.

As we look ahead into 1940 -- we are so eager to continue to tell out the Gospel story faithfully while there is still time -- for our hearts almost fail us! Anti-christian forces are rampant in the world -- and they are strong! We wonder, CAN we continue sending out the Gospel during this year -- through all the five Sunday months -- and through the long summer? Then we realize that this is God's work -- and though we are so weak, He is strong. As we look to Him He will sustain and guide, and will undertake. Our hearts are comforted and strengthened by the following verses:

"The eyes of the Lord are upon the righteous, and His ears are open unto their cry" -- Psa. 34:15.

"Behold the eye of the Lord is upon them that fear Him, upon them that hope in His mercy" -- Psa. 33:18.

"Not by sight, nor by power, but by My Spirit, saith the Lord" -- Zech. 4:6.

So 1940, we salute you, and go forth to meet you in His strength! This world -- in its darkness and anguish -- needs Christ! We again dedicate ourselves to the preaching of the Gospel -- praying "Let Thy mercy, O Lord, be upon us, ACCORDING AS WE HOPE IN THEE" -- Psa. 33:22.

In His strength,

Director.

TITLES IN THIS SERIES

The Evangelical Matrix
1875-1900

The Formation of
A Fundamentalist Agenda
1900-1920

■ 18. Joel A. Carpenter, ed.
*The Bible in Faith and Life,
as Taught by James M. Gray*
New York, 1988

■ 19. Mark A. Noll, ed.
*The Princeton Defense
of Plenary Verbal Inspiration*
New York, 1988

■ 20. *The Victorious Life:
Messages from the Summer Conferences*
Philadelphia, 1918

■ 21. Joel A. Carpenter, ed.
Conservative Call to Arms
New York, 1988

■ 22. *God Hath Spoken: Twenty-five Addresses
Delivered at the World Conference on
Christian Fundamentals, May 25- June 1, 1919*
Philadelphia, 1919

Fundamentalism Versus Modernism
1920-1935

■ 23. Joel A. Carpenter, ed.
*The Fundamentalist -Modernist Conflict:
Opposing Views on Three Major Issues*
New York, 1988

■ 24. Joel A. Carpentar, ed.
Modernism and Foreign Missions:
Two Fundamentalist Protests
New York, 1988

■ 25. John Horsch
Modern Religious Liberalism: The Destructiveness
and Irrationality of Modernist Theology
Scottsdale, Pa., 1921

■ 26. Joel A. Carpenter,ed.
Fundamentalist vesus Modernist
The Debates Between
John Roach Stratton and Charles Francis Potter
New York, 1988

■ 27. Joel A. Carpenter, ed.
William Jennings Bryan on
Orthodoxy, Modernism, and Evolution
New York, 1988

■ 28. Edwin H. Rian
The Presbyterian Conflict
Grand Rapids, 1940

Sectarian Fundamentalism
1930-1950

■ 29. Arno C. Gaebelein
Half a Century: The Autobiography of a Servant
New York, 1930

■ 30. Charles G. Trumball
Prophecy's Light on Today
New York, 1937

■ 31. Joel A. Carpenter, ed.
Biblical Prophecy in an Apocalyptic Age:
Selected Writings of Louis S. Bauman
New York, 1988

■ 32. Joel A. Carpenter, ed.
Fighting Fundamentalism:
Polemical Thrusts of the 1930s and 1940s
New York, 1988

■ 33. *Inside History of First Baptist Church, Fort*
Worth, and Temple Baptist Church, Detroit:
Life Story of Dr. J. Frank Norris
Fort Worth, 1938

■ 34. John R. Rice
The Home — Courtship, Marriage, and Children: A
Biblical Manual of Twenty -Two Chapters
on the Christian Home.
Wheaton, 1945

■ 35. Joel A. Carpenter, ed.
Good Books and the Good Book: Reading Lists by
Wilbur M. Smith, Fundamentalist Bibliophile
New York, 1988

■ 36. H. A. Ironside
Random Reminiscences from Fifty Years of Ministry
New York, 1939

■ 37 Joel A. Carpenter,ed.
*Sacrificial Lives: Young Martyrs
and Fundamentalist Idealism*
New York, 1988.

Rebuilding, Regrouping, & Revival
1930-1950

■ 38. J. Elwin Wright
*The Old Fashioned Revival Hour
and the Broadcasters*
Boston, 1940

■ 39. Joel A. Carpenter, ed.
*Enterprising Fundamentalism:
Two Second-Generation Leaders*
New York, 1988

■ 40. Joel A. Carpenter, ed.
Missionary Innovation and Expansion
New York, 1988

■ 41. Joel A. Carpenter, ed.
*A New Evangelical Coalition: Early Documents
of the National Association of Evangelicals*
New York, 1988

■ 42. Carl McIntire
Twentieth Century Reformation
Collingswood, N. J., 1944

■ 43. Joel A. Carpenter, ed.
The Youth for Christ Movement and Its Pioneers
New York, 1988

■ 44. Joel A. Carpenter, ed.
The Early Billy Graham:
Sermons and Revival Accounts
New York, 1988

■ 45. Joel A. Carpenter, ed.
Two Reformers of Fundamentalism:
Harold John Ockenga and Carl F. H. Henry
New York, 1988